Listen My Children

The Maclay Sixth Grade
Collegiate Poetry Course

Charles E. Moore

Order this book online at www.trafford.com
or email orders@trafford.com

Most Trafford titles are also available at major online book retailers.

Author Credits: Thanks to the Maclay School

Printed in the United States of America.

ISBN: 978-1-4669-7524-8 (sc)
ISBN: 978-1-4669-7525-5 (e)

Trafford rev. 01/09/2013

Trafford PUBLISHING® www.trafford.com

North America & international
toll-free: 1 888 232 4444 (USA & Canada)
phone: 250 383 6864 ♦ fax: 812 355 4082

CONTENTS

DEDICATION

With both gratitude and regard
This book is dedicated to

Mrs. Lou Lewis,

"Golden in the heydays"
of her Sixth Grade student's eyes,
and mine,

And also to my daughters

Amelia,

A Fifth Grade teacher of delightful excellence,
and

Meredith,

Who I hope will find in her life
Her own happy poetry.

—CM

LISTEN, MY CHILDREN

"Listen, my children, and you shall hear, of the midnight ride of Paul _____." (Who? Fill in the blank.)

All right! Way to go! So you got that one! How about "Ay, tear her tattered ensign down, long has it waved on high…"? Yes, you probably do know that it was written by Oliver Wendell Holmes in 1830, as part of an outburst of public objection to the proposed "scrapping" of our famous frigate, the *U.S.S Constitution*, "Old Ironsides."

Now then, try this: "When I was young and easy, under the apple trees…" What? Where? Who wrote those lines? And when?

HER TATTERED ENSIGN

It is nice to know about "what."   And "where." And a bit of "who," too. It is always nice, and fun, to know a few lines of poetry, even if you do not know the whole poem. Those lines can remain with you your entire life, and surface in your thoughts suddenly, like a submarine or a diver or a cork, up from the depths, bringing their whole world from maybe long, long ago to whatever it may be that you are doing when they suddenly pop up in your brain.

There are, of course, innumerable poems that you will discover for yourself, and by learning one, or even a bit of one, you will forever have the gift of certain words that will apply to all sort of things and events that will happen to you. Sometimes they may be just fragments, like some of my examples, which may be only a part of a longer poem. But even the fragments will make you smile as you remember them, and add a richness to your moment, and therefore to your life, when they come to surface.

Besides, over the last 600 years and more that the English language has evolved, it has been thanks to poets like those we will read that it has developed a richness for which it is famous among world languages. You will meet over time favorite poets of your own, and favorite fragments and whole poems that will add to your appreciation of whatever you do, because poems and poetry put the best of what we are into such memorable words.

This collection contains examples that have struck my own fancy all my life. They are not all, to be sure, "children's poems," but they and others are very much worth your hearing or reading at any early age, even if you think you will never remember anything about them. Some are easy, and some are hard. I have tried with each poem to help you, in my own way, to think about them and begin to understand them better.

Nor, by the way, should the gentlemen among you forget that deftly quoting a line or two of poetry, appropriate of course to the fair occasion and lady, may much brighten her esteem for you. As for you "fair ladies," beware, on the other hand, of the motives of young gentleman who whisper too many such "sweet nothings" in your ear.

But never mind. Beyond such trivial admonitions poetry is for the soul, so "let us go there, you and I…when the sunset is spread out against the sky…"

GEOFFREY CHAUCER (1340-1400)

All languages have their writers of songs, their poets. When the English language first began, it was born out of earlier forms of languages that had been brought to the British islands by various invaders. There was Latin, mixing and mingling for over four hundred years with the language we call Gaelic, which was spoken originally on those far-away (from Rome) misty, almost magical lands. There was a kind of German, brought over by the Angles and Saxons from the southern shores of the Baltic Sea; Norse as a result of the invasions of England by the Vikings between 700 and 1000 AD; and French from the "Norman Conquest," when King William of Normandy conquered the Britons in 1066 at the Battle of Hastings.

THE KNIGHT'S TALE

The beginnings of English, as we know it, arose from all of these different ways of speaking, picking up here a fragment, there a word, and forming these finally into patterns of speech and grammar that would blossom with _____(who?).

Why, of course, Geoffrey Chaucer, who with Shakespeare 200 years later might almost be said to have "invented" our language, and the way we use it. But even before Chaucer, poets were merrily scribbling away, and in an "English" that 700 years later we can pretty much recognize and understand. What is this unknown poet of that early time saying?

Summer is icumen in,

Lhudé sing cuccu…

Or, as you might say, "Hurrah! Summer is coming! School's out! I'm going to sing like a cuckoo"…and your parents might think you have become one.

Yes, it was Chaucer who sent our language, and the way we told stories and wrote our poetry, off into the future to become English as we know it, complete with more than 450,000 words to choose from.

Has anyone seen the movie "The Knight's Tale"? This is actually the name of one of Chaucer's stories, but the film is not like his story at all. In fact I think it highly unlikely that Chaucer himself ever ran about in the woods and roads stark naked, as in the movie. Chaucer was a diplomat, in fact, holding important positions such as serving as an ambassador from England to France and Italy. He learned in his travels some new ways of writing poetry, and furthermore took the unprecedented step of writing in the local language of common people, English, rather than the more acceptable French or Latin. By doing so, he gave our language its life. He is a real "Blast from the Past," and besides, his stories are lots of fun.

Chaucer's greatest and most famous collection of stories is "The Canterbury Tales." In these tales a number of people get together to go on a "pilgrimage" to the great cathedral at Canterbury. Their journey together is like a vacation, and as they go along, each tells a story for the others to hear, all for entertainment.

Listen! Here is his Prologue, or introduction, to these wonderful tales.

WHAT IS
   A 'PROLOGUE'?
            (HINT: 'PRO' MEANS 'BEFORE'
                   'LOGOS' IS GREEK FOR 'WORD')

The Prologue to *The Canterbury Tales*
(Geoffrey Chaucer, 1340-1400)

DOES THIS
SOUND LIKE
THE MODERN
WORD 'LIQUOR'?

Whan that Aprille with his shoures soote   (WHEN, APRIL, SHOWERS, SWEET)

The droghte of Marche hath perced to the roote, (DROUGHT, HAS, PIERCED, ROOT)

A 'ZEPHER'
IS A
GENTLE
BREEZE

And Bathed every veyne in swich licour,   (VEIN, SUCH, MOISTURE)

Of which vertu engendred is the flour;   (POWER, COMES FORTH, FLOWER)

What Zephirus eek with his swete breeth (GOD OF THE WINDS, SWEET, BREATH)

HAVE YOU
EVER HEARD
OF A 'HEATH'?
IT IS LIKE A
MOOR.

Inspired hath in every holt and heeth   (WOOD, FIELD)

The tendre croppes, and the yonge sonne, (TENDER, SEEDLINGS, YOUNG, SUN)

IN THE SPRING
THE SUN IS IN
THE CONSTELLATION
ARIES, 'THE RAM'

Hath in the Ram his halfe cours y-ronne. (RAM= SPRING, COURSE, RUN)

And smale fowles maken melodye,   (SMALL, BIRDS (FOWLS), MELODYE)

That slepen al the night with open ye, (SLEEP, ALL, EYE)

WHAT BIRD
SLEEPS WITH
ITS EYES OPEN?

(So priketh hem nature in hir corages), (PROMPTS, HER, DESIRES)

Than longen folk to goon on pilgrimages,(PEOPLE LONG TO GO ON)

WE KNOW
THIS WORD
AS 'COURAGE',
BUT IN CHAUCER'S
TIME IT MEANT
'DESIRE' AND 'DETERMINATION'

And specially, from every shires ende   (COUNTY'S, END)

Of Engelond, to Canterbury they wende... (WEND THEIR WAY, GO)

3

Terms on p. 70

WILLIAM SHAKESPEARE (1564-1616)

Who can remember when they first heard the name "Shakespeare"?

I knew the name perfectly well by the time I was eleven, "young and easy under the apple trees," when thumbing through a big book I had of *Ripley's "Believe It or Not,"* I discovered that Shakespeare's name could be spelled more than a dozen different ways. Maybe, also, I first heard it in conjunction with someone crying out, "To be or not to be," clapping their hands to their forehead and looking as if they might faint. Or maybe when someone was teasing me and said "Romeo, Romeo, wherefore art thou my sweet Romeo?" Or maybe around Halloween when we all said "Double trouble, boil and bubble..."

HAWK MEETS HANDSAW

In any event, we all know Shakespeare almost from the cradle. There never was, and I dare say there will never be again, anyone who has contributed all by himself so much to the English language. Innumerable words and phrases and lines from his plays and poetry are so much a part of our everyday speech, and we accept them so commonly, that we hardly remember that he actually invented them. "It's all Greek to me," he said, and we say it still when confronted with something we absolutely cannot understand. One of my own favorites, not so much quoted perhaps but which I love to say in place of saying that something happens only every now and then, is: "When the wind is southerly I know a hawk from a handsaw." (See "Hamlet," Act 2, scene 2.)

Shakespeare wrote during the reign of Queen Elizabeth the First, when there was a great flowering, a bursting forth like spring, of poetry, and fine language, and much else. A New World, America, was beginning to be more widely known, explored, and even settled by daring, swashbuckling, sea rovers such as Sir Walter Raleigh and Sir Francis Drake. Shakespeare was expanding the horizons of language, discovering its new possibilities, with the same sort of adventurous spirit as Raleigh and Drake in their adventures around the world. Shakespeare, aside from the poetry and songs contained in his plays, took the sonnet and gave it a new form, which we admire and use to this day.

And what, you might ask, IS a sonnet? Let me put it this way: it is a little poem that contains fourteen lines, with five accents in each line, making its little statement in a compact and beautiful fashion. The Italians "invented" the sonnet in the 14th century, with a rhyme scheme of ABB ABB ABB ABB AA, the "Italian sonnet." Shakespeare gave it a rhyme scheme of ABAB CDCD EFEF GG, adding his own genius to its beauty. Together with his plays, his sonnets are very important parts of what we consider the treasures of the English language.

We love sonnets themselves in no small measure, one might almost say, because of Shakespeare. Here are some that you might enjoy sampling. They are, by the way, lovely for quoting to a girlfriend! (As for you girls, be careful of those young men who start quoting them, for they might want to be rewarded with a kiss!)

WHAT IS A SONNET?
HOW MANY LINES
DOES IT HAVE?
    A.) 6
    B.) 10
    C.) 22
    D.) 14

SHAKESPEARE SONNET
By William Shakespeare, 1564 – 1616

IN THIS PART
OF THE
SONNET IS
SHAKESPEARE

A.) COMPLAINING
B.) WHINING
C.) UNHAPPY
D.) ALL OF
    THE ABOVE

When, in disgrace with Fortune and men's eyes,

I all alone beweep my outcast state,

And trouble deaf heaven with my bootless cries,

And look upon myself and curse my fate,

Wishing me like to one more rich in hope,

Featured like him, like him with friends possessed,

Desiring this man's art, and that man's scope,

With what I most enjoy contented least;

Yet in these thoughts myself almost despising,

Haply I think on thee; and then my state,

Like to the lark at break of day arising

From sullen earth, sings hymns at heaven's gate;

For thy sweet love remembered such wealth brings

That then I scorn to change my state with kings.

BOYS! TAKE IT
FROM ME. THIS
IS THE POEM TO
READ ALOUD ONE
DAY TO A FAIR
MAIDEN! IT WILL
WIN HER HEART
EVEN IF YOU ARE
NOT WEARING A
DR. SEUSS HAT...

WOW! DOES
HE LIKE HER
A LOT?
    OR
        NOT?

GIRLS! BEWARE OF
    YOUNG MEN WHO READ
    THIS ALOUD TO YOU!
    (ESPECIALLY IF HE IS
        WEARING A DR. SEUSS HAT)

Terms on p. 71

JOHN DONNE (1572-1631)

Now here, I tell you, is a hard poet for your ears and heart and brain.

First as a man, then as a priest in the English Church, and then as Dean of St. Paul's Cathedral, Donne spoke words that powerfully touch upon our own modern doubts and feelings. It is John Donne, after all, who said what you will hear so many times over in your own life that "No man is an island…" In other words, the life of each and every one of us is important to us all as a whole, and the death of another diminishes us all.

A case can be made that Donne, perplexed by questions of Life and Death, and all the strange contradictions in which we find ourselves, is one of the first

NO MAN HERE

of what we might call the "modern poets." Do you not, yourself, ever wonder about why and what you are? Do you ever think it a curious thing that, in this great universe, you happen to be here at all? Is it not both a miracle and an amazement? What does your life mean, and what can you make of it?

These were the sorts of questions Donne asked and tried to answer in the poems and sermons that he wrote. In his own lifetime his poetry was little known, but he was very great at sermons, and people loved to hear him. It was really only about a hundred years ago that an American poet (whom we will read later), T. S. Eliot, more or less "rediscovered" Donne. Eliot was struck by Donne's curious use of words and expressions in which big and little, life and death, knowing and not knowing were all tangled up, not unlike how people were beginning to think in modern times.

The words Donne used to express himself will seem strange to you. It is hard sometimes to understand their meaning, harder than with Shakespeare and Chaucer who sound to us more straightforward and direct. But that is a part of Donne that is so interesting. The style with which he wrote is almost an expression in itself of his own doubts and confusions, which he sought to lay to rest by putting his Faith and Hope in God.

In the poem "Death be not Proud," he is determined to convince himself that "Death" is nothing, it is just like "sleep," and that if we are not afraid of it, then Death itself has no meaning. And anyway, he adds, in "Eternitie," or what we might call "Heaven," there is no further death, but only everlasting life. Death therefore is itself Dead, and we are the victors over it.

Well, does not this seem comforting? Of course. And it probably gave Donne a good deal of comfort too.

In a famous story that comes down to us from one of Donne's contemporaries, before he died, Donne called for candles and a shroud (what they used to wrap a dead person in), then had himself wrapped in the shroud, with just his pale face showing, and with his eyes closed, he had his portrait painted.

6

WHY MIGHT DEATH
BE 'PROUD' ANYWAY ?
A.) BECAUSE HE LOOKS GOOD
    IN BLACK
B.) BECAUSE DEATH JUST GOT
    A NEW SCYTHE.
C.) BECAUSE HE
    KNOWS HE
    WILL GET US ALL
    IN THE END
D.) HE GOT A
    HIGH MARK
    ON THE
    FINAL EXAM
    IN
    'DESTRUCTION
    101'

IS THIS POEM A
SONNET ?
    A.) YES
    B.) NO
    C.) YES AND NO
    D.) DON'T KNOW

Sonnet: Death Be Not Proud
(John Donne, 1572-1631)

Death be not proud, though some have called thee

Mighty and dreadfull, for, thou art not soe,

For, those, whom thou think'st, thou dost overthrow,

Do not, poor death, nor yet canst thou kill mee.

From rest and sleepe, which but thy pictures bee,

Much pleasure, then from thee, much more must flow,

And soonest our best men with thee doe goe,

Rest of their bones, and soules deliverie.

Thou art slave to Fate, Chance, kings, and desperate men,

And dost with poyson, warre, and sickness dwell,

And poppie, or charmes can make us sleepe as well,

And better than thy stroake: why swell'st thou then?

One short sleepe past, wee wake eternally,

And death shall be no more: death, thou shalt die.

IS DONNE
SAYING ALL
THESE THINGS
TO MAKE
DEATH SOUND
A.) LESS FEARFUL
B.) MORE FEARFUL
C.) LIKE WATCHING
    T.V.
D.) LIKE SLEEP
E.) LIKE A.
    AND D.

WHEN YOU
'SWELL' AND
GET ALL
PUFFED UP,
IT IS USUALLY
WITH
A.) HAMBURGERS
B.) VICIOUS BLOAT
C.) PIZZA
D.) PRIDE
E.) MOSTLY D, BUT SOMETIMES
    WITH A. AND C., AND
    ALMOST NEVER WITH B.

HOW IS DEATH
'KILLED' EVEN IF
WE SEEM TO
DIE ?
(HINT: SEE THE
LINE ABOVE)

7

Terms on p. 72

JOHN MILTON (1608-1674)

Everyone (almost) knows about "Paradise Lost," and Satan, and Beelzebub, and the "fallen Angels," and maybe even the fact that Milton wrote his great epic poem "to justify the ways of God to Man."

But except for scholars, I do not myself know anyone who has ever read "Paradise Lost," or for that matter much Milton at all. He is rather "out." He is less read than Donne, I would say, by far.

Yet it was not always so. For 250 years Milton was revered and read as "the Greatest," esteemed even beyond Shakespeare for his lofty ideals and poetic vision. His words seemed to people to come down from some high mountain, noble, and richly contrived in the very finest garments that the English language could put on.

SATAN'S FALL

It was T. S. Eliot (once again!), and a certain shift in our attitudes toward language that came about in the early 20th century, that caused Milton to go out of fashion, so to speak. Suddenly he seemed too flowery, too wordy, maybe even too thoughtful. In a word he became, almost overnight, BORING. But even so, he remains perched on his mountaintop, one of the greatest poets in our literature.

After all, he did write the greatest Epic of the English language, even if he may never have quite "justified the ways of God to Man." And he wrote it at a moment in English history when a great Civil War was being waged between the Puritans, led by Oliver Cromwell, and the Royalists, led by King Charles the First. Who won the war? Well, the Royalists ultimately defeated Cromwell's forces, but not before Charles had lost his head, by which I mean, of course, had had it chopped off by Cromwell. Throughout the English Civil War, Milton, a Puritan, supported Cromwell, and perhaps visualized Cromwell's revolt against the King as being a little like Satan's revolt against God. Since Milton was on the side of the rebels, it is not surprising that he felt such a great need to "justify" himself.

In his great description of the clash between the legions of Heaven and Hell, and the rebellion of the Angels who joined Satan against God, Milton created a poem that gripped everyone's imagination in the same way that "Star Wars," with Darth Vader starring as Beelzebub, gripped our own imaginations. There is a mighty clash of Good and Evil, and since there were no movie theaters in the days of Milton, people relied upon the richness of the written word, and their own listening ears and imaginations.

You may never read "Paradise Lost" in all its 12 books (!) but you can at least appreciate the drama of the moment when the "fallen" angels are plotting against God.

For this, and many other works and poems, Milton was venerated. He finally went blind, bore his fate with dignity, and spent his last years dictating poems to his daughters. We like to think of them as beautiful girls, who adored their old Dad.

'PARADISE LOST' IN THE 17th CENTURY WAS AS BIG A "HIT" AS WAS 'STAR WARS' IN THE 20th. IN 'STAR WARS' WHO WAS 'SATAN'?

A.) LUKE SKYWALKER
B.) R2D2
C.) OBI-WON-KANOBI
D.) DARTH VADER

WHAT DOES THIS DESCRIBE?

A.) DISNEYWORLD
B.) A TEA PARTY
C.) HELL
D.) OZ

From "Paradise Lost"
By John Milton, 1608 – 1674

Him the Almighty Power
Hurled headlong flaming from the ethereal sky,
With hideous ruin and combustion, down
To bottomless perdition, there to dwell
In adamantine chains and penal fire,
Who durst defy the Omnipotent to arms.
Nine times the space that measures a day and night
To mortal men, he, with his horrid crew,
Lay vanquished, rolling in the fiery gulf,
Confounded, though immortal. But his doom
Reserved him to more wrath; for now the thought
Both of lost happiness and lasting pain
Torments him; round he throws his baleful eyes,
That witnessed huge affliction and dismay.
Mixed with obdurate pride and steadfast hate.
At once, as far as Angel's ken, he views
The dismal situation waste and wild.
A dungeon horrible, on all sides round,
As one great furnace flamed; yet from those flames
No light; but rather darkness visible
Served only to discover sights of woe,
Regions of sorrow, doleful shades, where peace
And rest can never dwell, hope never comes
That comes to all, but torture without end
Still urges, and a fiery deluge, fed
With ever-burning sulphur unconsumed.
Such place Eternal Justice has prepared
For those rebellious; here their prison ordained
In utter darkness, and their portion set,
As far removed from God and the light of Heaven
As from the center thrice to the utmost pole.
Oh how unlike the place form whence they fell!
There the companions of his fall o'whelmed
With floods and whirlwinds of tempestuous fire,
He soon discerns; and, weltering by his side,
One next himself in power, and next in crime,
Long after known in Palestine, and named
BEELZEBUB. To whom the Arch-Enemy,
And thence in Heaven called SATAN, with bold words
Breaking the horrid silence, thus began: . . .)

"HIM" WAS WHO? AND WHO ELSE, FLUNG FROM HEAVEN, LOST PARADISE?

A.) SATAN
B.) LUCIFER
C.) BEELZEBUB
D.) THE DEVIL
E.) ALL OF THE ABOVE

WHERE IS 'PERDITION'? IS IT...

A.) HEAVEN
B.) A LOUD SHOPPING MALL
C.) HELL

AND SO NOW, LED BY SATAN, THE FALLEN ANGELS BECOME TERRORISTS, AND BEGIN TO PLOT THE OVERTHROW OF HEAVEN.

JOHN DRYDEN (1631-1700)

In the hundred years after Queen Elizabeth's death in 1603 and Shakespeare's in 1616, poetry began to take on a different sort of sound. The Elizabethans, like Chaucer long before, had loved a rather flowery use of the language, taking delight in exploring its possibilities. Poetry sometimes did not even rhyme, as in the "free" verse of Shakespeare. But as the century wore on, through Milton and with the English Civil War Onen the middle of it, the "rules" for writing poetry became less free. More and more, poetry had to be written in a certain way, with a rhyming scheme if it was to be appreciated as "true poetry," and aspire to greatness.

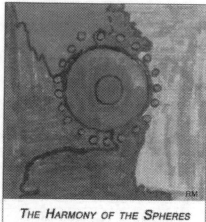

THE HARMONY OF THE SPHERES

Times and ideas change. The world seen by the children of one generation is not the same world as the parents lived in, unless you lived in a faraway, colonial backwater, like Anne Bradstreet, who lived in the Massachusetts Bay colony. She died in 1672 and is described as "having written the first good poems in America." That she did so is all the more interesting because in those days a woman, and a Puritan at that, was not supposed to dabble in literary affairs at all.

But back in England, after the Civil War was over in 1660, the Monarchy was restored. Charles II, the son of Charles I, who had had his head so rudely chopped off (the shirt he wore, with the bloodstains still on it can yet be seen in a museum in England) by Cromwell, became King of England.

And John Dryden became the King of poetry.

Well, maybe no one very much reads Dryden now either. But if Milton, or Shakespeare, were the golden names of English poetry, Dryden was the silver. He exerted a tremendous influence on the way poetry was to develop, how people came to think about it, and the forms it would take. He was widely read. Other writers and poets "sat at his feet," to listen to his opinions about poetry and literature, and to strictly abide by them. They thought that if they did, they would have a chance at becoming great, too.

His rules became their laws. Poetry now became not so much a matter of feeling, but of thinking, and it had to be written in a certain way, according to a certain strict etiquette. Maybe it was because Charles II, who had lived so long in France, brought to England all sorts of new codes and fashions of behavior. In any case, swashbuckling adventuring in poetry, or on the high seas that the Elizabethans enjoyed, was out, and decorum and proper forms were in.

By the time of his death in 1700, Dryden had set the standard that poetry should be governed, like everything else, by reason, order, and authority. God is all of this, and so should kings and poets reflect the same. In his "Song for St. Cecilia's Day," Dryden praises the ordered notes and "heavenly harmony" of music. That is, of course, the music of his time, and NOT "acid Rock"! And he describes how God the Maestro, his baton in hand, created the world from "jarring atoms" right up to the noblest work of all: Man.

...AND WHO IS SHE? SHE IS THE PATRON SAINT OF MUSIC, THAT'S WHO...

IN LONDON FROM 1683 to 1703 THERE WERE CELEBRATIONS IN HER HONOR WITH CONCERTS AND SONG CONTESTS

DOES THIS SOUND
A.) NEAT
B.) TIDY
C.) ORDERED
D.) A MESS?

A SONG FOR ST. CECELIA'S DAY
John Dryden (1631-1700)

THIS IS THE FIRST STANZA OF A SONG WRITTEN BY DRYDEN FOR THE OCCASION

From harmony, from heavenly harmony
This universal frame began:
When nature underneath a heap
Of jarring atoms lay,
And could not heave her head

AND NOW WHAT HAPPENS?

The tuneful voice was heard from high:
"Arise, ye more than dead."
Then cold, and hot, and moist, and dry,
In order to their stations leap,
And Music's power obey.
From harmony, from heavenly harmony,
This universal frame began:
From harmony to harmony,
Through all the compass of the notes it ran,
The diapason closing full in man.

WHAT IS A 'DIAPASON'?

IT IS A SCALE, LIKE A LADDER, EACH RUNG EQUALLY DISTANT FROM THE OTHER, OR LIKE MUSIC NOTES THAT ASCEND HARMONIOUSLY UPWARD OR DOWNWARD

IN A CHAIN, OR DIAPASON, IN WHAT ORDER FROM TOP TO BOTTOM WOULD YOU RANK
A.) A BEAN
B.) A HUMAN
C.) A ROCK
D.) A ROACH

ALEXANDER POPE (1688-1744)

Who, as a small, frail little boy, but with a great big brain, was brought in fact to "sit at the feet" of the great poet of the age, John Dryden? And who, young though he was, saw how very much Dryden was admired, and said to himself that someday he, too, would be surrounded by just such admirers? Who perceived at that early age that a great poet might possess great power? Who noted that John Dryden was the Poet Laureate of all England and was heaped with praise and even the possibility of riches?

OH HAPPY GROTTO!

You are right. It was Alexander Pope. Such a little fellow he was, and ill formed by a hunched back. But he had a huge ambition and a poetic genius that was exactly tailored to the new forms, as Dryden was laying them down, of writing poetry. And Dryden, almost first among all the poets and writers, including even Shakespeare and Milton, had made a lot of money as a result of his verse and writings. Young Master Pope determined that he would follow in those footsteps and become "the Greatest."

Well, he was not "the greatest," but he became very great, and did make a lot of money in the writing of his poems, and also from his translations, eagerly read, of *The Iliad* and *The Odyssey*. He took his money and built himself a charming house on the banks of the Thames, upstream from London, where he had constructed for himself a real *grotto*, a sort of secret cave. These sorts of "follies" were popular in those days among adults, who could pretend they were magical and mysterious. You cannot think otherwise than that Pope loved being a famous and wealthy poet.

The 18th century is called "The Age of Reason." It was a time when great and reasonable ideas about man and society and governments were being discussed, written about, and finally, at the end of the century, put into practice in the new nation that called itself the United States of America. Reason, rather than passion and emotion, offered mankind a path upwards towards a better way of life.

One might say that Pope, in his poetry, was almost too "reasonable." In his poetry, just as in the world of Lords and Ladies, Squires, Gents, and peasants, every word and person had to be exactly in the right place, everything had to "fit," and every line had to rhyme with the line above it: the "heroic couplet."

Pope who has come to stand for the "heroic couplet," in fact. Who knows why it is called "heroic"? Maybe it took a sort of "heroism" to be able to make up all those rhymes, where every syllable was in its perfect rank like soldiers in line, and the last word of every line rhymed with the one above it. This went beyond Dryden in being "reasonable," for sure, but people loved it. And beyond this, Pope's rhymes were so very clever, and his words so very witty that he could write about anything. One of his most famous "mock Epics" was about a wayward lock of a young lady's hair, a subject utterly trivial, but which he made great by his clever and poetic genius. .

To our ears, Pope's poetry cries out for a bit more honest emotion, just a little passion, please. But he was marvelous at what he knew how to do, as this fragment from the "Essay on Man" and his translation of *The Iliad* demonstrate.

KNOW THYSELF
Alexander Pope (1688 – 1744)

Know then thyself, presume not God to scan;
The proper study of mankind is man.
Placed on this isthmus of a middle state,
A being darkly wise and rudely great:
With too much knowledge for the Sceptic side,
With too much weakness for the Stoic's pride,
He hands between; in doubt to act or rest,
In doubt to deem himself a God or Beast,
In doubt his mind or body to prefer;
Born but to die, and reasoning but to err;
Alike in ignorance, his reason such
Whether he thinks too little or too much:
Chaos of thought and passion, all confused;
Still by himself abused, or disabused;
Created half to rise and half to fall;
Great Lord of all things, yet a prey to all;
Sole judge of truth, in endless error hurled:
The glory, jest, and riddle of the world!

what does this mean? why not?

what is an 'isthmus'?

and 'a middle state' between what and what?

what is a 'sceptic'?

← AN ISTHMUS

what is a 'Stoic'?

name this creature:
A. A TURTLE
B. AN ALIEN
C. AN ANGEL
D. MAN

How many 'beats', or stresses are there to each line?

Are these 'heroic couplets?

why 'heroic?

13

Terms on p. 73

THOMAS GRAY (1716-1771)

Then, by the last half of the 18th century, everyone began to think that a little emotion, although not quite going so far as to permit "passion," might be allowed. After all, people do not merely *think* things, they also *feel* them.

Take Thomas Gray, for example. You can think about Death all you want, and be very reasonable about it too, but when you get right down to it you discover you have feelings about it, fear maybe, the sadness of it, its inevitability, and so on, which cannot be denied. His "Elegy in a Country Churchyard," published in 1751, is his famous meditation on this subject. It was a huge hit in the 18th century, and it remains one of the most famous poems in the English language for its eloquent expression of feeling.

RUDE FOREFATHERS SLEEPING

Thomas Gray was a nice man, very studious and scholarly. "A quiet sort of man was he," timid in public, but among his friends a good companion, with a gentle sense of humor and a twinkle in his eye. He had no interest in fussy "follies" like Grottos, or in the money and acclaim that so beguiled Alexander Pope. He was happy to be left alone to quietly pursue his literary researches at Pembroke College, Cambridge, where he was both a Master (teacher) and a scholar. Here he lived the quiet life of a literary "nerd," somewhat withdrawn, enjoying his studies of English literature, making translations from other languages into English, and writing beautiful letters to his friends.

In all his life he wrote less than 1000 lines of poetry, a very small output for someone who nonetheless made so great a name for himself as a poet. His poems seem rather like himself: gentle, quiet, thoughtful, even melancholic, but also now and again revealing flashes of humor, as in his "Ode on the Death of a Favourite Cat."

Unlike the rather hard, cold edge that Pope was so brilliantly, and ruthlessly, capable of using in his "heroic couplets," Gray's sentiments, and indeed his very words, are soft, gentle, and musing, following one another almost like those elegiac cows, each one after the other quietly wending their way back to the barn in the soft twilight of a fading day. Even in just the beginning lines of "The Elegy" you can see how much it is about mood and feeling. Just as Pope's poetry captures people's minds, Gray's captures our hearts.

It is this appeal to the heart, and the beauty of the words chosen for that purpose, that makes Gray so great a poet despite the small quantity of poetry that he wrote. His was a new voice, one that gave expression not just to great subjects of mind and myth, but to our own voice within us, musing on life and death, natural beauty, friendship, and so on even down to the death of a favorite cat.

Gray broke the mold that Dryden and Pope had created. He led the way, despite his withdrawn modesty, into a whole new world of poetry where feelings became supreme. It was from Gray that the so-called "Romantic Poets" of the next generation were to derive their inspiration, producing poets and poems that still define the way we think (and feel!) about poetry itself.

KIDS OFTEN HAVE THESE TOO

IN THE MIDDLE AGES, BEFORE CLOCKS, THE 'CURFEW' WAS A BELL THAT WAS RUNG TO TELL THE PEOPLE IT WAS TIME TO RETIRE

WHAT IS AN 'ELEGY'?
A.) A SORT OF CHEER AT A FOOTBALL GAME
B.) A POLITICAL SPEECH
C.) A PRAISE AND LAMENT FOR SOMEONE DEAD
D.) A HARANGUE

WHAT IS A 'HARANGUE'?

AND WHAT AN ORANGOUTANG?

An Elegy Written in a Country Churchyard
Thomas Gray (1716-1771)

The curfew tells the knoll of parting day,
The lowing herd winds slowly o'er the lea,
The plowman homeward plods his weary way,
And leaves the world to darkness, and to me.
  Now fades the glimmering landscape on the sight,
And all the air a solemn stillness holds;
Save where the beetle wheels his droning flight,
And drowsy tinklings lull the distant folds.
  Save that from yonder ivy-mantled tow'r
The mopeing owl does to the moon complain
Of such as, wand'ring near her secret bow'r,
Molest her ancient solitary reign.
  Beneath whose rugged elms, that yew-tree's shade,
Where heaves the turf in many a mould'ring heap,
Each in his narrow cell for ever laid,
The rude forefathers of the hamlet sleep.

IS THIS POEM
A.) LOUD
B.) FUNNY
C.) QUIET

OR IS IT
A.) LIGHT
B.) DARK
C.) COLORFUL

WHO ARE THESE PEOPLE? WHERE DO THEY SLEEP?

WHAT IS THE DIFFERENCE IN THE SETTING OF THIS POEM AND THAT OF 'PARADISE LOST'?

QUICK! WHO WROTE 'PARADISE LOST'?

WHAT IS THE DIFFERENCE BETWEEN THE COLOR 'GRAY' AND 'GREY'?

NONE. YOU CAN SPELL THE COLOR EITHER WAY

WILLIAM BLAKE (1757-1827)

But first there was an exceptional interlude, in the form of a living, breathing, true-to-life "Visionary."

Now what is a "Visionary"?

"ME? BURNING BRIGHT?"

If you think it is someone who has "visions," you are absolutely correct. On the other hand, having visions is not so simple. The only "visions" most of us have are the ones that Hollywood makes up for us. Blake, on the other hand, seemed to have true visions every now and then throughout his life, starting when he was only eight and saw God looking in at him through a window. Hurrah for Blake! He was not only a talented poet, but a brilliant artist who was wonderfully capable of drawing what must have been some of his visions, Angels and Archangels, God and the Devil, gloriously on paper. No one has ever illustrated so beautifully the splendor of the words he could also write

Yes, Blake stands alone, all by himself. He is certainly not a part of that "Classic" set of writers and poets who, like Dryden and Pope, looked back to the great Roman authors, Virgil and Horace for example, to copy. His artistic world derived from his visions, which drove his mind and imagination towards their expression on paper. No one, in his time, could quite understand him, for when you don't have visions yourself you are a little uncertain of those who do. Anyone can relate to Gray and trust him, because inside ourselves we can see that we share his sentiments almost exactly. But who could share Blake's visions of what he called "the New Jerusalem," or for that matter even his "Songs of Innocence"?

To be frank, to people of the 1780s, including I feel pretty sure George Washington, Blake seemed crazy.

We are now, let us hope, a bit more tolerant. Perhaps, in a way and in time, Blake has helped us to become so. We can now value talent and genius even in people who may indeed see visions or, as we tend to somewhat disrespectfully call them now, hallucinations. Did you ever see the film "A Beautiful Mind," about the Princeton mathematician who won the Nobel Prize despite his (terrible) hallucinations?

Happily for him, and us, Blake was somehow able to control his "visions," expressing them merely in his poetry and paintings. Otherwise he was thought of as an eccentric, a bit of an "odd duck." We can be grateful, for had he not seemed harmless, he might well have been thrown into "Bedlam," that terrible place in London where the "insane" were locked away, to be publicly mocked and ill-treated. Had this happened, and had Blake not written poetry as a result, we would have indeed lost a "beautiful mind," one possessed with a burning, fierce imagination like no other.

Nor would we have had "Tyger, Tyger," one of the greatest poems of them all.

WHY DO YOU THINK
BLAKE CHOSE A
TIGER TO WRITE ABOUT?
WHY NOT
A CHICKEN
A WORM
A PEANUT?

THE TYGER
By William Blake, 1757 – 1827

IS THIS A
POEM ABOUT
MORE THAN
A TIGER?
WHO?

Tyger! Tyger! Burning bright
In the forests of the night,
What immortal hand or eye,
Could frame thy fearful symmetry?

In what distant deeps or skies
Burnt the fire of thine eyes?
On what wings dare he aspire?
What the hand dare seize the fire?

WHAT
'FIRE'
IS THIS?

And what shoulder, and what art,
Could twist the sinews of thy heart?
And when thy heart began to beat,
What dread hand? And what dread feet?

What the hammar? What the chain?
In what furnace was thy brain?
What the anvil? What dread grasp
Dare its deadly terrors clasp?

HINT: BLAKE WAS
AS GREAT AN
ARTIST AS HE
WAS A POET.
SEE THE IMAGE
DRAWN BY
BLAKE BELOW.
WHO IS IT? WHAT
IS HE
MEASURING?
TO DESIGN AND
CREATE WHAT?

When the stars threw down their spears,
And water'd heaven with their tears,
Did he smile his work to see?
Did he who made the Lamb make thee?

Tyger! Tyger! Burning bright
In the forests of the night,
What immortal hand or eye,
Dare frame thy fearful symmetry?

CAN
YOU
GUESS, OR
KNOW,
WHY
Lamb BEGINS
WITH A CAPITAL L?

HINT: WHO IS
CALLED 'THE
Lamb OF
GOD'?

Terms on p. 77

ROBERT BURNS (1759-1796)

I have a friend who is not only Scottish, but very Scottish. He is quite typical of his doughty breed in being very proud of his Scottish ancestry and home. In the garden behind his Mom's and Dad's house, he showed me the little stream, where, for the first time ever, in 989 A.D., his forbears defeated in a bloody battle the Norse invaders who had wrought so much havoc across the land. "This," says Colin (his chest slightly puffing up), "is where the Battle of (whatever) took place, and afterwards the murderous Vikings never troubled us again." He "rolled" his Rs with vigor, giving impressive authority to the word "murderous," which contains all of two. Naturally, listening to him, I wanted to be Scottish myself.

A WEE SLEEKIT MOUSIE

Of course, and most proudly, Colin's home in Ayrshire was just up the road a few miles from where "Robbie" Burns lived and wrote his poetry.

In Scotland that, indeed, is a name to conjure with! By which I mean, of course, that in that name lies real magic. No people could be more proud of one of their poets than the Scottish are of Burns. He is quoted here, he is quoted there, he is simply quoted everywhere. On his birthday, "Burns Suppers" are given far and wide, large and small, across the land to toast the memory of Robbie Burns. In honor of his poem "To a Haggis" (a kind of oat meal and offal sausage stuffed in a sheep's stomach, and Scotland's nearly "National Dish") the Haggis is borne in on high, to the thrilling trill of a bagpipe. The Haggis is "addressed," everyone standing respectfully. Speeches are given recounting the life and exploits of Burns, his poems read aloud, and his life celebrated with what the Scots might call a "wee libation." For Burns was all for life, ladies, whisky, and rhyme. He was rather shocking in fact, especially in a time when manners and morals were rather more decorous than nowadays. He was sort of like a "Rock Star" of today. But he left us with immortal lines of poetry. And so the Scotch, and we too, toast indeed the life and times of Robbie Burns! You go to a "Burns Supper" to share with everyone else the rollicking good fun which is also the legacy of Burns, who comes down to us larger than life. Everyone is happy and jolly and *bonnie* and *brae,* and surely rolls their Rs if they possibly can, and goes home warm with all the festivity.

It is all good fun. But Burns was, as well, a great poet, who lived life in a rich and merry way himself. Some dour folk might say he lived too fast and merry, and so died young at the age of only 36. But for sure his poems live on, and grow even better. They have about them so much of the Scots' good humor and wise understanding that to this day they enrich the Scottish people and nation. What is more, Burns was perhaps the first to write in the common spoken idiom of the people. To our ear it sounds very much an almost foreign dialect of English, with its rolling rhythms and many words deriving from Gaelic that we have never heard at all, but yet remain alive in Scottish diction to this day. In his times, just a bit after Pope, many questioned whether his poetry was poetry at all. But we know it is, and full rich and *braw* it be, I might add.

Have you ever heard this one about the wee mousie? I have left out a few stanzas, but it contains a famous line about mice and men, and their plans.

Does Burns want to hit the little mouse with a paddle?

TO A MOUSE
By Robert Burns

Wee sleekit, cow'rin, tim'rous beastie,
O, what a panic's in thy breastie!
Thou need na start awa sae hasty,
Wi bickering brattle!
I wad be laith to rin and chase thee,
Wi murdering pattle!

SLEEK COWERING TIMID

RUSHING SCURRY
LOATH RUN
PADDLE

Is Burns sad that he might frighten the mouse?

I'm truly sorry man's dominion
Has broken Nature's social union,
An justifies that ill opinion,
Which makes thee startle
At me, thy poor earth-born companion.
An fellow mortal!

Is he glad to give the mouse a little corn?

I doubt na, whyles, but thou may thieve:
What then? Poor beastie, thou maun live!
A daimen icker in a thrave
'S a sma request:
I'll get a blessin wi the lave,
An never miss't!

NOT SOMETIMES
MUST
EAR OF CORN 24 SHEAVES OF CORN
SMALL
REMAINDER

What sad thing happened?

Thou saw the field laid bare and waste,
And weary winter comin fast.
An come here, beneath the blast,
Thou thought to dwell,
Till crash! The cruel coulter past
Out thro thy cell.

PLOUGHSHARE
NEST

Can a mouse predict his future?

But mousie, thou art no thy lane,
In proving foresight may be vain:
The best-laid scheme o mice an men
Gang aft agley,
An lea'e us nought but grief an pain,
For promis'd joy,

ALONE

GO ASTRAY

Can a human? And what does a human have to deal with that a mouse does not?

Still thou art blest, compar'd wi me!
The present only toucheth thee:
But och! I backward cast my e'e,
On prospects drear!
An forward, tho I canna see,
I guess an fear!

EYE

19

WILLIAM WORDSWORTH (1770-1850)

Well, yes, all those "feelings" did break loose. And more hugely than anyone would have ever imagined.

The French Revolution, in July, 1789, was as shocking to the ordered world of the 18th century as 9/11 was to us. All those Lords and Ladies, living their ordered lives, where everything and everyone was in its proper place, suddenly found their heads dropping into a basket beneath the blade of *Madame La Guillutine.* "Reason" was tossed aside. Raw passion and spilt blood, prevailed.

On the other hand, particularly at first, there were many who welcomed the downfall of the old tyrannies, and eagerly looked forward, as had already happened in the new United States of America, to a government based on the individual rights of every citizen. In France the cry was for "*Liberté, Egalité, Fraternité*": liberty, equality, and fraternity.

PROTEUS

Young William Wordsworth was one of those who wanted to see the old ways done away with, at least until the excesses of the Revolution, and the dictatorship of Napoleon which followed it, disillusioned him. Even then, his spirit remained revolutionary, but directed into poetry, not politics. It was Wordsworth who fully opened the floodgates of feeling, pouring forth in words his passion for man as an individual, for the freedom of man, and also for the mystery of man in the midst of nature. Among great events, such as the French Revolution, or great floods, volcanos, earthquakes, seas, and storms, what was man? Did he not, in truth, seem puny and frail beside the power of the forces amidst which he dwelt?

With Wordworth, and his great poem called "The Prelude," begun in 1798, the "Romantic Rebellion" was upon us. The sedate, "classical" past seemed but quaint and old-fashioned by comparison to the power of the new and mighty feelings that suddenly dominated the thoughts and works of writers, poets, and painters everywhere. Pope would have been shocked. Even the mild-mannered Gray, who played a role in starting it all, would have been amazed. Poetry no longer spoke in dainty rhymes, but in the words of common men.

Wordsworth lived a long time, but the best of his poetry was written before 1807. In it he demonstrated his faith in the dignity of individual people. His poetry leaves a deep mark that remains etched into our feelings about our modern world still. His passionate sensitivity to nature, in both its calms and its cataclysms, is a part of the reason why we, even in this 21st century, are so sensitive to nature's beauty and meaning.

Feel for yourself, as you read, how deeply Wordsworth embraced this world that he, and we, live in. As part of mankind, he said, we are a wonderful part of the magic and mystery of it all.

And so we are, don't you think?

20

QUIZ: THIS POEM IS A SONNET BECAUSE IT HAS (FILL IN THE BLANK) ___ LINES.

AND HOW MANY ('DUM-DE-DUM DE-DUM) BEATS ARE THERE TO EACH LINE ?

A.) 9

B.) 3

C.) 6.25

D.) 5

Sonnet: The World Is Too Much With Us
William Wordsworth (1770-1850)

VERY FAMOUS LINE MEANING WHAT ?

AND WHAT HAVE WE GIVEN OUR 'HEARTS AWAY' TO...

The world is too much with us, late and soon,

Getting and spending, we lay waste our powers:

Little we have in nature that is ours;

We have given our hearts away, a sordid boon!

This sea that bares her bosom to the moon;

The winds that will be howling at all hours,

And are up-gathered now like sleeping flowers,

For this, for everything, we are out of tune;

It moves us not.- Great God! I'd rather be

A Pagan suckled in a creed outworn;

So might I, standing on this pleasant lea,

Have glimpses that would make me less forlorn;

Have sight of Proteus rising from the sea;

Or hear old Triton blow his wreathed horn.

WOULD YOU SAY THIS IS MORE TRUE NOW THAN 200 YEARS AGO? YES ___ NO ___

WHAT IS A 'LEA'. HAVE YOU EVER STOOD ON ONE ?

WHO IS PROTEUS ?

WHO IS 'OLD TRITON' ?

HE WAS A GREEK GOD OF THE SEA

HE, TOO, WAS...

WHAT WOULD THIS HORN MOST LIKELY BE WREATHED WITH ?

A.) POISON IVY

B.) SEAWEED

C.) CHRISTMAS TREE LIGHTS

D.) POPCORN

WHY WHICHEVER ?

GEORGE GORDON, LORD BYRON (1788-1824)

Then along came Byron, the very mention of whose name would cause young ladies' hearts to flutter, if not fully faint into a graceful swoon, requiring that they be briskly fanned, and smelling salts called for.

For sure. Byron was a different sort of poetic bird. He was, in fact, perhaps the first poetic Mega-bite, genuine, breathe-your-last gasp Super-Star. Everything he did and said caused everyone, and mostly young ladies (which means a lot), to "Ooooh" and "Ahhhhh" and flutter their eyelashes and get hot and slightly damp. They all hoped that Byron might come galloping over the horizon and carry them off. Even Moms fluttered at the thought of him, although for form's sake they had to deplore even the idea that their daughters could be so seduced by a poet who was, after all, so scandalous.

BYRON ABOUT TO WRITE A POEM ABOUT HIMSELF

Byron, in fact, did bring "Scandal" to poetry, almost single-handedly making poetry and poets a wildly popular notion. Yes, he was scandalous, but his scandals were performed with great wit and stylish flare. Besides, his poetry was in its way greater than just "great," it was supercagilisticfragaloptimostest. Which is to say it was nothing at all like Dryden, or Gray or Wordsworth, poets who for all their intensity and brilliance in expressing their thoughts and feelings lacked, even so, what Byron so richly possessed: Glamour and Passion.

Yes, Byron basically created the idea of the poet's being both glamorous and passionate, more than anyone else in those days when there were no movie stars. All the more exciting, he was also a Lord of the realm. Even if his family had fallen on hard economic times, so what? Nobles were the Superstars of that age. He grew up in a real castle, went to the best schools, Harrow and Cambridge, and wrote poems that even before he was 20 were thought shocking. In fact, they were attacked with such vigor that Byron left England in 1809, and spent three years traveling in Portugal, Spain, Albania, and Greece, which were then very exotic places to visit. The reasons he left England, and the places he visited, made him seem all the more a "romantic" figure.

On his return to England in 1812, Byron published the first two episodes of his long poem called "The Pilgrimage of Childe Harold." And who, really, was this Childe Harold fellow? He was Byron, who cast himself as the handsome, exotic, romantic and slightly flawed hero of his own poem. Byron looked and acted the part. He did surprising and daring things, like swimming across the Hellespont, which in the days of ancient Greece only heroes had ever done. He gloried in the freedom and independence of his own spirit. He dressed the part of the romantic brigands of Albania and Greece, and young ladies fell madly in love with him.

Finally, having created such an overpowering image of himself, he had to live up to it. Of course, he continued to write his wonderful poems, full of wit and dash, in praise of individual freedom. More, he gave up his life to his beliefs. He went again to Greece where he lent his great name to the cause of Greek freedom from the long rule of that country by the Ottoman Turks. And there he died, probably of malaria.

WHO IS THIS 'CHILDE HAROLD' PERSON ?

HE WAS A GOOD FRIEND OF WHO ?

A.) THE PRESIDENT
B.) KUBLA KHAN
C.) SHELLEY
D.) OZYMADIAS
E.) MILTON

And I Have Loved The Ocean
From *Childe Harold,*
George Gordon, Lord Byron (1788-1824)

HINT:
SEE ESSAY ON OPPOSING PAGE

There is a pleasure in the pathless woods,
There is a rapture on the lonely shore,
There is society where none intrudes,
By the deep sea; and music in its roar:
I love not Man the less, but Nature more,
From these our interviews, in which I steal
From all I may be, or have been before,
To mingle with the Universe, and feel
What I can ne'er express, yet cannot all conceal.

Roll on, thou deep and dark blue ocean – roll!
Ten thousand fleets sweep over thee in vain;
Man marks the earth with ruin – his control
Stops with the shore, - upon the watery plain
The wrecks are all thy deed, nor doth remain
A shadow of man's ravage, save his own,
When, for a moment, like a drop of rain,
He sinks into thy depths with bubbling groan,
Without a grave, unknell'd, uncoffin'd, and unknown.

DOES THE OCEAN TO BYRON STAND FOR

A. THE AWESOME POWER OF NATURE
B. A PLACE TO SWIM
C. BOTH OF THE ABOVE

A FAMOUS LINE : DOES BYRON SEEM TO LIKE 'WHICH' OF THE BELOW BETTER :

A. MEAN PEOPLE
B. PEOPLE
C. CATS
D. TREES, LAKES, MOUNTAINS, SKIES

And I have loved thee, Ocean! And my joy
Of youthful sports was on thy breast to be
Borne, like thy bubbles, onward from a boy
I wanton'd with thy breakers – they to me
Were a delight, and if the freshening sea
Made them a terror – 'twas a pleasing fear,
For I was as it were a child of thee,
And twisted to thy billows far and near,
And laid my hand upon thy mane – as I do here.

WHO IS 'HE' THIS DEAD BODY. WHOEVER IT WAS DOES THAT PERSON, TO BYRON, ADD UP TO VERY MUCH COMPARED TO THE OCEAN ?

EVEN SO, DOES BYRON FEEL CLOSE.... EVEN A PART OF THE OCEAN ? HAVE YOU EVER FELT SO IN ITS WAVES ?

23

PERCY BYSSHE SHELLEY (1792-1822)

Shelley was another Romantic poet filled with, almost dominated by, his passions. He and his wife Mary were friends with Byron. In 1816 they rented with other somewhat exotic and passionate people an old villa, the "Villa Diodati," in the mountains of Switzerland. It was there, in a right merry mood one wild and stormy night, that Byron, Dr. Polidori, and the Shelleys challenged each other to write a ghost story. Everyone more or less copped out, except for Mary Shelley who wrote *Frankenstein*, a wild work (as you know) of romantic horror that has become far more popularly known than even the poems of Byron and Shelley themselves. In that dramatic tale, which she so brilliantly contrived, Mary Shelley said a great deal about a real

NOTHING BESIDE REMAINS

portion of what we call the "Romantic Movement." If man dares, in his pride, to tamper with the tremendous forces of nature and God's plan, what terrors might be let loose on the earth? Mary Shelley's story of Frankenstein, whom she also called "the Modern Prometheus," is a frightening fable, and remains even today a powerful warning of what we too might harmfully let loose in our exploration of new technologies such as cloning or atomic energy.

But back to Percy Shelley, who is almost the veritable-all-by-himself spokesman and archetypal poet of all the romantic poets. Like Byron he grew up in a privileged environment, went to and was thrown out of England's best schools, and at a young age was already writing brilliant poems. But whereas Byron both created and even enjoyed promoting his image as the romantic poet-hero, Shelley was sincerely and passionately devoted to his cause of individual freedom. Shelley, in fact, sometimes seems so enthusiastic over "the rights of man" that he appears almost to want to get rid of any rules at all. He was sort of a wild thing.

His poetry, even so, is some of the most beautiful and deeply felt in the English language. His passion lies right at the surface of his every beautiful word. He wrote all sorts of poems, sonnets, odes and long dramatic poems. He was deeply sensitive to the cruelty of individual freedom's being denied, and people's dying chained to dungeon walls. Shelley is filled with darkness and with light. But if the dark is foul, the light is pure, and as brilliant as the words themselves. His poem "Adonais" is a beautiful elegy written after the early death of Keats, whom we will read next. In that poem he famously wrote "Life, like a dome of many colored glass stains the white radiance of eternity." It is that "white," almost white-hot, "radiance" that consumed Shelley. It also made him one of the very greatest poets of our language.

There are some scholars who might guess that Shelley had an unconscious, barely suppressed fascination with death. He seems to wish almost to join himself indeed to that "white radiance of eternity," where his spirit will soar forever free.

Perhaps it is fitting that he died sailing, alone but free. Was there a storm? Perhaps pirates set upon him. In any case he drowned, and his body was found days later, washed ashore. He had in his pocket a book of Keats's poetry. His friends built a great bonfire on the beach, and cremated him. And so his body became a part of the air.

24

WHAT IS THE
   DIFFERENCE BETWEEN
      A ONE 'L' AND A TWO 'L'
         TRAVELER? A 'LAMA' AND
      A 'LLAMA' AND IS THERE A 'LLLAMA'?

HINT:

Ozymandias
Percy Bysshe Shelley (1792-1822)

WHAT IS A 'VISAGE'?

I met a traveller from an antique land
Who said: Two vast and trunkless legs of stone
Stand in the desert. Near them, on the sand,
Half sunk, a shattered visage lies, whose frown,
And wrinkled lip, and sneer of cold command
Tell that its sculptor well those passions read
Which yet survive, stamped on these lifeless things,
The hand that mocked them, and the heart that fed:
And on the pedestal these words appear:
"My name is Ozymandias, king of kings:
Look on my works ye Mighty, and despair!"
Nothing beside remains. Round the decay
Of that colossal wreck, boundless and bare
The lone and level sands stretch far away.

WHY IS THIS WORD NOT 'DESSERT'?

IS THIS A NICE KING?

WHERE IN THE WORLD DO YOU THINK OZYMANDIAS WAS KING?

WAS HE A POWERFUL KING, OR WEAK?

WAS HE PROUD OR WAS HE MEEK?

WHAT HAPPENED TO HIM, FINALLY, THAT HAPPENS TO EVERYONE? (FILL IN THE BLANKS) HE _ _ _ _.

AND HIS WORDS ERASED BY 'THE SANDS OF _ _ _ _ _?'

SAMUEL TAYLOR COLERIDGE (1772-1834)

We have all heard of "The Rhyme of the Ancient Mariner," and that albatross which became such a curse, and of "Kubla Khan," who "a mighty pleasure dome decreed." And then there is "Christabel," a phantom tale of demon-magic and mystery, meaning...what?

Well, no one quite knows what it all means. But everyone knows that it is powerful stuff, filled with haunting images and lines that, once read, almost no one ever forgets. It is in the weird strangeness of his visions that we discover what is the best of Coleridge, and what makes him, for all of his otherwise highly appreciated intellect, one of the greatest of the "Romantic Poets."

Yes, yes, he had some bad toothaches and took

LIGHTNING OVER THE ALPH

opium, a hard drug readily available in those days, which eased pain and caused also dreams and stupors. Yes, yes, "Kubla Khan" was thought one of those dreams which, when Coleridge woke, he quickly started to commit to poetry until someone famously interrupted him by knocking on his door, and the remembrance of his vision passed away. Many of Coleridge's poems were not quite finished. But the fact that they were but fragments of something intended to be longer almost adds to their magic and power.

Brilliant though he was as a writer, speaker, critic, and poet, Coleridge longed to be "complete" himself, but was disappointed in many things: family life, love, and even finally in his close friendship with Wordsworth. Is Coleridge himself "the ancient mariner," cursed to roam the earth unfulfilled in his deepest desires? Did he wish he had the magical power of "Kubla Khan," so that he might create for himself a "Xanadu," that gorgeous place of his imagination, "where Alph, the sacred river ran"?

"Whatever," as one might say today. Or else, maybe, "Who knows what lurks in the mysterious shadows of the mind?" This brings us to another point about the Romantic movement. Beyond its passionate feeling for Nature, and its devotion to the ideal of individual freedom and the dignity of the common man, lay also a fascination in the unknown, darker depths of the human mind. In the time of Pope every word and every thing was in its proper place and order. Now, at the very beginning of the 19th century, there came this revelation, almost like a lightning bolt. In a blinding flash poets and artists were struck by the awareness that in nature, and in man too as a part of nature, there exists a powerful tendency, and even temptation, towards upheaval, disorder, and chaos sometimes beyond anyone's ability to understand or control. How frightening this was, but how exciting too.

Coleridge's poems capture that magic, that fear, and that excitement better than the poetry of any of the other Romantics. He shows us "the dark side," weaving a spell of words magical in themselves. The best of his poems are like strange flashes of light briefly illuminating all that is dark and unknown in each of our brains.

QUESTION: DOES A POEM HAVE TO HAVE A
MEANING? FOR EXAMPLE, LIKE 'OZYMANDIAS,'
WHICH TELLS HOW TIME BRINGS DOWN EVEN
THE MOST POWERFUL. DOES 'KUBLA KHAN' HAVE
SUCH A MEANING,
OR DOES IT
SAY SOMETHING
ELSE ABOUT
WHAT A
POEM CAN
BE?

Kubla Khan
Samuel Taylor Coleridge (1772-1834)

In Xanadu did Kubla Khan
A stately pleasure-dome decree:
Where Alph, the sacred river, ran
Through caverns measureless to man
    Down to a sunless sea.
So twice five miles of fertile ground
With walls and towers girdled round:
And there were gardens bright with sinuous rills,
Where blossomed many an incense bearing tree;
And here were forests ancient as the hills,
Enfolding sunny spots of greenery.

Through wood and dale the sacred river ran,
Then reached the caverns measureless to man,
And sank in tumult to a lifeless ocean:
And 'mid this tmult Kubla heard from far
Ancestral voices prophesying war!
    The shadow of the dome of pleasure
    Floated midway on the waves,
    Where was heard the mingled measure
    From the fountain and the caves,
It was a miracle of rare device,
A sunny pleasure-dome with caves of ice!...

I would build that dome in air,
That sunny dome! Those caves of ice!
And all who heard should see them there,
And all should cry, Beware! Beware!
His flashing eyes, his floating hair!
Weave a circle round him thrice,
And close your eyes with holy dread,
For he on honey-dew hath fed,
And drunk the milk of Paradise.

DID
THIS
PERSON
EVER
REALLY
EXIST
HISTORI
    C
    A
    L
    L

?Y

IS THIS A
STRANGE
PERSON
OR
NOT?

QUIZ: DOES THIS POEM
A. TEACH A LESSON
B. MAKE A POINT
C. SIMPLY DESCRIBE
    A PLACE
    IMAGINED
D. PROVIDE A MEANS
    FOR COLERIDGE
    TO PASS SOME
    TIME SINCE IN HIS
    DAY T.V. DID NOT
    EXIST.

IF YOU CHOSE 'C.' YOU
ARE CORRECT, I DO
BELIEVE. IF YOU WERE
TO DESCRIBE THIS POEM
(CIRCLE THE ANSWERS
YOU THINK MOST
APPROPRIATE) AS

HAPPY   SCARY   WEIRD   SILLY
MYSTERIOUS   MERRY   GLOOMY   STUPID
AN ADVERTISEMENT   FOR 'PLEASURE-DOMES
LIKE A DREAM   HOT   COLD
                IN BETWEEN

Terms on p. 82

JOHN KEATS (1795-1821)

And finally, in the midst of all this, there was Keats. You cannot help but love him, and probably more than any other of the poets of that romantic age. No, he was not an "exotic" like Byron, or burning like a hot flame for the sake of his ideas like Shelley. "Nature," and man's place in it, were not for him the important issues they were for Wordsworth. He did not possess the intellect or colorful dreams of Coleridge. He wrote his poetry simply for the sake of its beauty, and the ideas followed.

"Wow!"

Keats appeals to us not only out of the genius of his beautiful poetry, but because in his short life his struggles were so highly personal. His heart did not lie, really, with great issues, except perhaps that "beauty is truth, truth beauty," but with those small, personal afflictions that torment anyone: finding and making a living, hoping to marry his girl friend Fanny Brawne, and keenly longing to make his mark as a poet.

There was one very great issue with which Keats all too early had to struggle, and that was Death. In those days tuberculosis was a dreadful disease, for which there was no cure. People hardly spoke its name. But everyone knew that the mark of death was upon you if and when you coughed up some bit of bright, red blood. Keats, age 22, but having for some months felt unwell, coughed into his handkerchief, and saw that terrible spot. He knew immediately that the days of his life were numbered, and said, after closely examining the spot, "it is my death warrant."

Reviews of his poetry had been disappointing, for reviewers still looked back to the previous, more strict standards that had defined poetry's forms and ideals. Their negative reviews were for Keats bitter disappointments, causing him almost to despair. But he wrote on, determined to give the world the lovely poems that were in his heart. Of all the romantic poets, his was the loneliest struggle, racing against his own death.

Finally, in 1820, his illness gripping him ever more closely, he did the only thing his doctors knew to advise. He went to Italy, where the warm climate might help to prolong his life. He arrived there weak and exhausted in the company of his friend, the painter Joseph Severn. They took rooms in Rome, overlooking the "Spanish Steps." There, nursed by his friend, he coughed and bled his life away far from home and Fanny Brawne. He was only 25.

"The Keats House" is still there, maintained by the Italian government as a historical monument to one of the greatest of the English poets. It is kept just as it was when Keats died there, and you may one day want to visit it. You will see the plaster "Death Mask" made of Keats' face immediately after he died. It is a handsome and noble countenance. A visit there, to stand in those very rooms, is for many like making a pilgrimage.

The tragedy of his death, his youth, his struggles, and the beauty of his poetry, which Shelley himself so much appreciated, make Keats for me both the most touching and also the greatest of the Romantic poets.

WHO IS THIS CHAPMAN FELLOW?

HOW OLD WAS KEATS WHEN HE DIED? HINT
A. 23
B. 34
C. 26
D. 29

ON FIRST LOOKING INTO CHAPMAN'S HOMER
John Keats (1795-1821)

GEORGE CHAPMAN 1559-1634, FIRST TRANSLATED HOMER'S ILIAD FROM GREEK INTO ENGLISH.

WHERE DO YOU THINK IS THIS 'REALM OF GOLD'?
A.) IN AFRICA
B.) IN A SHOPPING-MALL
C.) ON MARS
D.) IN KEATS' IMAGINATION

Much have I travell'd in the realms of gold,
And many goodly states and kingdoms seen;
Round many western islands have I been
Which bards in fealty to Apollo hold.
Oft of one wide expanse had I been told
That deep-brow'd Homer ruled as his demesne;
Yet did I never breathe its pure serene
Till I heard Chapman speak out loud and bold;
Then felt I like some watcher of the skies
When a new planet swims into his ken;
Or like stout Cortez when with eagle eyes
He star'd at the Pacific—and all his men
Look'd at each other with a wild surmise—
Silent, upon a peak in Darien.

DOES HE MEAN THAT CORTEZ WAS OVERWEIGHT? DOES HE MEAN CORTEZ AT ALL?

WHY APOLLO?

WELL, WAS HE THE GREEK GOD OF LIGHT, REASON, & LEARNING, OR NOT?

NO, 'STOUT' ALSO MEANS 'STRONG' OR 'STURDY'—AND IT WAS 'NOT' CORTEZ WHO FIRST DISCOVERED THE PACIFIC OCEAN, BUT BALBOA

WHICH IS WHERE?

AND WHAT IS A 'DEMESNE'?

WHICH SHOWS THAT A GREAT POET CAN MAKE A MISTAKE, FOR IT WAS BALBOA WHO STOOD ON THAT 'PEAK IN DARIEN', WHICH WE NOW CALL PANAMA

YOU COULD LOOK IT UP IN THE DICTIONARY... BUT IT WILL DO IF YOU SAY 'IT IS A GREEK TERM FOR 'AN AREA OF LAND WHERE EVERYONE LIVES UNDER THE SAME RULER OR LAW.

Terms on p. 82

EDGAR ALLEN POE (1809-1849)

After such floodgates of feeling had been opened by the poets of the Romantic Rebellion (they had rebelled, as we have seen, against the staid, intellectual poetic forms insisted upon by Dryden and Pope), where, one might ask, could poetry go after that? No one in 1825 would have been able to answer that question. But then, as always happens, along came someone who took poetry a peculiar but meaningful step further. Poe led it even beyond those passions of the spirit that Shelley held so dear, and into what we might call the subconscious. Into the unknown. Into our darkest fears. Into the macabre.

RAVEN QUOTHING

Edgar Allen Poe was the first American poet, except maybe for Longfellow, who was enormously popular in both England and America, and gained an international reputation. Beyond that, he particularly impressed the French, who are usually not very impressionable. Longfellow's verse was very pretty and musical to the ear. For example, just say the opening line to one of his famous poems, "Under the spreading chestnut tree the village smithy stands," but its pleasant rhythm and beauty does not compare, especially to our modern ears, to the sinister atmosphere of Poe's poems.

The Romantic poets explored and revealed in their poetry their inner selves, their hopes and aspirations both for themselves and the world. Poe delved deeper into the dark corners of the human heart. In those corners he found terrible visions, ghosts, apparitions, warnings, and threats. Who knows what the Raven means when it says "Nevermore"? But in that word, and particularly as Poe used it in his poem over and over, it sounds like doom itself. Poe gave voice to the blackness that can lodge within the depths of our souls.

He was not, accordingly, well received in his time, when America was blossoming with optimism. Poetry was supposed to be pretty, and maybe uplifting, too. It was for that reason that Longfellow basked in great success as a poet, and made a comfortable, even wealthy living from his writing. Poe was essentially impoverished throughout his life, and did himself further harm by becoming an alcoholic.

But of the two, Poe and Longfellow, it was Poe who more profoundly affected the direction poetry was to take in the future. He became very popular in France, a country that has always taken pride in its ability to create new directions in art of any kind. After the defeat of Napoleon at Waterloo in 1815, the French went through a bitter time, and perhaps for that reason the dark words of Edgar Allen Poe appealed to them. In any case, Poe became a great example to the French, and their poets in the generation after him followed in his footsteps. Poets became interested in weird, dark symbols, scarcely understandable to "normal" people and a far cry from the pretty world of Longfellow.

It is because of Poe that poetry remains tempted to give its voice to the bizarre and frightening feelings and fears that, down deep, everyone lives with to some degree. Poe brilliantly introduced us to those fears. Poets today continue to write of them, but none with quite the power that Poe possessed.

30

THE RAVEN
Edgar Allen Poe (1809-1849)

HAVE YOU EVER FELT 'DREARY' 'WEAK' & 'WEARY' IN ONE SINGLE LINE ALL AT ONCE?

Once upon a midnight dreary, while I pondered weak and weary,
Over many a quaint and curious volume of forgotten lore.
While I nodded, nearly napping, suddenly there came a tapping,
As of someone gently rapping, rapping at my chamber door.
"'Tis some visitor," I muttered, "tapping at my chamber door –
Only this, and nothing more."

WOULD YOU BE A LITTLE, OR A LOT, SCARED?

HAVE YOU EVER 'NODDED, NEARLY NAPPING'?

Ah, distinctly I remember it was in the bleak December,
And each separate dying ember wrought its ghost upon the floor.
Eagerly I wished the morrow; - vainly I had sought to borrow
From my books surcease of sorrow – sorrow for the lost Lenore –
For the rare and radiant maiden whom the angels named Lenore –
Nameless here for evermore.

WHAT DO YOU THINK HAPPENED TO HER?

HAVE YOU EVER FELT 'CREEPY IN A BLEAK DECEMBER, SITTING 'BY A DYING EMBER'?

And the silken sad uncertain rustling of each purple curtain
Thrilled me – filled me with fantastic terrors never felt before:
So that now, to still the beating of my heart, I stood repeating
"'Tis some visitor entreating entrance at my chamber door –
Some late visitor entreating entrance as my chamber door; -
This it is, and nothing more."

Presently my heart grew stronger; hesitating then no longer,
"Sir," said I, "or Madam, truly your forgiveness I implore;
But the fact is I was napping, and so gently you came rapping,
And so faintly you came tapping, tapping at my chamber door.
That I scarce was sure I heard you" – here I opened wide the door; -
Darkness there, and nothing more.

IS THIS A DREAM? DOES IT TAKE COURAGE TO OPEN WIDE THAT DOOR?

Back into the chamber turning, all my soul within me burning,
Soon again I heard a tapping somewhat louder than before.
"Surely," said I, "surely that is something at my window lattice;
Let me see then, what thereat is, and this mystery explore –
Let my heart be still a moment and this mystery explore; -
'Tis the wind and nothing more!"

IF THIS HAPPENED TO YOU, WOULD YOU SAY,
A. WOW!
B. YEOW!
C. HOLY COW!
D. MEOW

HAVE YOU EVER 'PERCHED AND SAT, AND NOTHING MORE, EVEN THOUGH NOT ON THE DOOR?

Open here I flung the shutter, when, with many a flirt and flutter,
In there stepped a stately raven of the saintly days of yore.
Not the least obeisance made he; not an instant stopped or stayed he;
But, with mien of lord or lady, perched above my chamber door –
Perched upon a bust of Pallas just above my chamber door –
Perched, and sat, and nothing more.

Then this ebony bird beguiling my sad fancy into smiling,
By the grave and stern decorum of the countenance it wore,
"Though thy crest be shorn and shaven, thou," I said, " art sure no craven.
Ghastly grim and ancient raven wandering from the nightly shore –
Tell me what thy lordly name is on the Night's Plutonian shore!"
Quoth the raven, "Nevermore!"

WHERE DOES PLUTO REIGN?
A. IN DISNEYWORLD
B. THE GREEK UNDERWORLD (HADES)
C. ON SATURN
D. BEYOND NEPTUNE
B. & D.

And the raven, never flitting, still is sitting, still is sitting
On the pallid bust of Pallas just above my chamber door;
And his eyes have all the seeming of a demon's that is dreaming,
And the lamp-light o'er him streaming throws his shadow on the floor;
And my soul from out that shadow that lies floating on the floor
Shall be lifted – nevermore!

DOES THIS RAVEN 'NEVER FLITTING, ALWAYS SITTING' FORESHADOW, TO POE, HIS OWN DOOM?

ALFRED LORD TENNYSON (1809-1891)

Born in the very same year, 1809, as Edgar Allen Poe, Tennyson could scarcely have been more different. For starters Tennyson lived twice as long as Poe. Tennyson became the Poet Laureate of England, honored, praised, and made a Baron by Queen Victoria, the first English writer to be honored thus. Poe died, probably of tuberculosis, wretchedly poor, an alcoholic, without praise and by some even reviled. The volume of work left by Poe was small compared to that of Tennyson, who wrote his first poem before he was five and then had 75 years in which he wrote many more.

GRIEVOUSLY WOUNDED

Tennyson was to England what Longfellow was to America: all honor and praise were theirs. Each mastered a certain poetic rhythm that was lovely in the ear, even if it sometimes sounded repetitious, and finally, maybe, even put you to sleep. Both men even looked as Poet Laureates should: distinguished, wise, and with very fine beards and noble brows. By comparison, Poe looked rather like a rat, or maybe a raven, thin and ravaged by disease and drink.

As poet Laureate, Tennyson was "the voice of the British nation." He was expected, when a great thing happened, to produce a great poem in honor of the event. And he did. His famous "Charge of the Light Brigade" is a splendid example of how he rose to the occasion, describing the courage of a cavalry charge into big guns that killed most of the horses and men, in a war England was fighting against Russia. He wrote, as well, a long retelling of the story of King Arthur and his Knights of the Round Table. He wrote wonderful verse about Ulysses and the Lotus Eaters. He was loved and much admired for a whole series of poems, which he called "In Memoriam," written after the youthful death of his closest friend. These poems enormously appealed to the Victorians, who lived closer to death than we because of the prevalence of so many diseases for which they had no cure. When Queen Victoria's own husband, Prince Albert, whom she dearly loved, died of typhoid fever, the Queen went into mourning for years, and her only consolation was reading "In Memoriam."

Yes, Tennyson dwelt, and wrote, in a lofty sphere, and on the whole avoided those dungeons of despair which so appealed to Poe's imagination.

On the other hand, if you look closely, you can see that Tennyson was not free of doubts and fears. Even though he lived in a world in which there was great hope for the future of mankind, and a great faith in what science and technology were creating, Tennyson could not fully embrace that optimism. He often felt very uncertain. He almost seemed to feel, sometimes, that there were great forces at work that could suddenly turn to evil. He was troubled that the wicked Modred does, in fact, defeat the good and great King Arthur, who is carried off near to death. Do you think it is Tennyson's hope that Arthur will recover, return, and his banner fly again to assert the ideals of the Round Table?

Tennyson, old and honored, died in his own castle, with the last light of a beautiful sunset flooding his room. Like Shelley and Keats, he defines our idea of a poet.

AND SO, IN THAT LAST GREAT BATTLE BY THE WESTERN, WINTER SEA, KING ARTHUR'S KNIGHTS ARE DEFEATED BY THE DARK FORCES OF THE TRAITOR, SIR MODRED. ARTHUR IS BADLY WOUNDED, 'UNTO DEATH,' BUT WITH THE LAST STROKE OF EXCALIBUR SLAYS MODRED. OF THAT GOODLY COMPANY OF ARTHUR'S ROUND TABLE ONLY SIR BEDIVERE IS LEFT...

From "The Passing of Arthur"
Alfred Lord Tennyson (1809-1892)

And slowly answer'd Arthur from the barge:
"The old order changeth yielding place to new,
And God fulfills himself in many ways,
Lest one good custom should corrupt the world.
Pray for my soul. More things are wrought by prayer
Than this world dreams of. Wherefore, let thy voice
Rise like a fountain for me night and day.
For what are men better than sheep or goats
That nourish a blind life within the brain,
If, knowing God, they lift not hands of prayer
Both for themselves and those who call them friend?
For so the whole round earth is every way
Bound by gold chains about the feet of God.
But now farewell. I am going a long way
With those thou seest—if indeed I go—
For all my mind is clouded with a doubt,
To the island-valley of Avilion:
Where falls not hail, or rain, or any snow,
Nor ever wind blows loudly; but it lies
Deep-meadow'd, happy, fair with orchard lawns
And bowery hollows crown'd with summer sea,
Where I will heal me of my grievous wound.

CAN YOU THINK OF AN EXAMPLE OF HOW "THE OLD ORDER CHANGETH"?

WHAT OTHER POET WROTE OF AN EVIL FORCE THAT BETRAYED GOOD AND WAS CAST FROM HEAVEN?

A. SHELLEY
B. MILTON
C. POPE
D. CHAUCER

WHAT IS THIS DOUBT?
A. ABOUT THIS WORLD
B. ABOUT HIS LIFE
C. ABOUT THE STRUGGLE BETWEEN GOOD AND EVIL
D. ALL OF THE ABOVE

WHAT KIND OF A PLACE IS THIS?

IS IT MOST LIKE
A. GEORGIA
B. DISNEY WORLD
C. A SORT OF PARADISE
D. MACLAY GARDENS

WHY DO WE HOPE ARTHUR WILL BE HEALED?

WELL, DO WE NOT NEED GOOD AND NOBLE LEADERS?

33

EMILY DICKINSON (1830-1886)

It was of great themes like the legend of Arthur that poets often wrote. And then, who came along to write about the littlest, tiniest things imaginable, things that strangely and beautifully contained in themselves whole universes?

Quite so, quite so. You are right. It is Emily Dickinson.

Could she ever have dreamed that she would become such a superstar? She would have been utterly astonished. I wonder how she would have handled all the fame she has now earned? Maybe it is just as well she was not put to the test, and died so long, really quite long, before she was ever discovered. As it was she did, after all, have a few of her poems published

LOOKING FOR SMALL THINGS

in her lifetime, but only after they had been altered and "improved" to better suit the public taste by the Editor of the magazine publishing them. Her short, little poems, he thought, were simply too far beyond the poetic conventions of the time. Their form was too quirky, and her feelings as she revealed them in her poetry so suddenly turned upon themselves, often within a single word, that readers felt almost disoriented. No, fame was never hers in her lifetime. But upon her death her sister found in her trunks sixty volumes, 1,775 poems, neatly tied together with twine.

Has there ever been a poet who is also more of a riddle than Emily Dickinson?

Born into comfort, she grew up in the pleasantly privileged atmosphere of her family's home in Amherst, Massachusetts, where her father was a professor at the college. On the surface of it, her girlhood was that of any normal young lady of the time. At age 17 she was looking forward to going to what amounted to "the Prom."

What happened we shall never know. But she suddenly gave up all social aspirations, withdrew from everyone and everything, and became perhaps America's most famous recluse. It was said that for fifteen years she never left her house, although sometimes, always dressed in white, she would be seen briefly in her garden. She never wrote about, or even hinted in her poetry, what had prompted this intense withdrawal. She died at age 56, after a life lived within the narrowest, self-imposed confinement, which she embraced with all the ardor of nuns who had made their holiest vows to God.

In Emily Dickinson's case her religion was her poetry, and her life lay within it. It was the outlet for the intensity of her feelings, which were passionately aroused by the smallest details of the life she experienced within the narrow perimeter of her home and garden. From the least thing and the tiniest sound she distilled revelations of sharp, concise profundity. She taught the world how, as they say, "less can be a great deal more."

It was not until 1955 that an accurate edition of her poems was finally published. By then she was already a Myth, and her poems had become Magic.

34

THE BRAIN IS WIDER THAN THE SKY

Emily Dickinson (1830 – 1886)

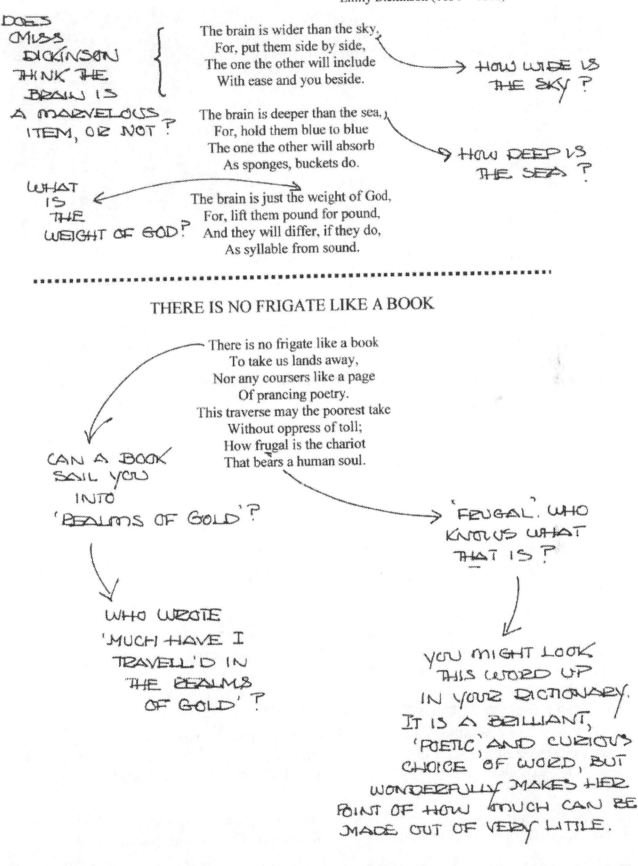

DOES MISS DICKINSON THINK THE BRAIN IS A MARVELOUS ITEM, OR NOT?

The brain is wider than the sky,
For, put them side by side,
The one the other will include
With ease and you beside.

HOW WIDE IS THE SKY?

The brain is deeper than the sea,
For, hold them blue to blue
The one the other will absorb
As sponges, buckets do.

HOW DEEP IS THE SEA?

WHAT IS THE WEIGHT OF GOD?

The brain is just the weight of God,
For, lift them pound for pound,
And they will differ, if they do,
As syllable from sound.

THERE IS NO FRIGATE LIKE A BOOK

There is no frigate like a book
To take us lands away,
Nor any coursers like a page
Of prancing poetry.
This traverse may the poorest take
Without oppress of toll;
How frugal is the chariot
That bears a human soul.

CAN A BOOK SAIL YOU INTO 'REALMS OF GOLD'?

WHO WROTE 'MUCH HAVE I TRAVELL'D IN THE REALMS OF GOLD'?

'FRUGAL'. WHO KNOWS WHAT THAT IS?

YOU MIGHT LOOK THIS WORD UP IN YOUR DICTIONARY. IT IS A BRILLIANT, 'POETIC', AND CURIOUS CHOICE OF WORD, BUT WONDERFULLY MAKES HER POINT OF HOW MUCH CAN BE MADE OUT OF VERY LITTLE.

35

Terms on p. 84

WALT WHITMAN (1819-1892)

Let me tell you that no one could have been more different from Emily Dickinson than Walt Whitman. Emily Dickinson lived out her life within a cloistered microcosm of her own making, deeply seen and acutely felt. Walt Whitman, on the other hand, threw open his arms, and embraced the whole world in a great bear-hug, with equal intensity. Emily's poems were diminutive, like fragments of shattered glass, but they focused on what she saw with all the power and heat of a magnifying lens concentrating the sun's rays to a tiny, white-hot point. Walt wrote large, his enthusiastic energy pouring forth onto page after page, covering the big world, which he quite considered "his," just as an overflowing river-torrent covers the land. She was tiny, dressed all in white. He was large, with a great beard, dressed in the clothes of a common workman.

THE EARTH IS SUFFICIENT.

Whitman, who had none of the "privilege" and security that surrounded Emily Dickinson, volunteered as a "Nurse" in the Civil War. There he was exposed every day to huge issues of Life, Death, and Suffering. He felt deeply about these issues, and about our country, too. He was a patriot, "All-American," in love with our people and our land in a way that no one has ever expressed before or since. In fact, he was in love with all people, all lands, with all possibilities, all hopes.

It did not matter to him what "path" he chose, for whatever his choice he would grasp it, rise to its occasion, impose himself upon it, and take it and make it proudly his very own. That, for Walt Whitman, was what life was all about, and he sang of it as a singer sings a song, with the volume turned up as high as it will go.

But wait! Pause a moment. Think, if you can, how Emily Dickinson and Walt Whitman did, after all, have something in common. Count to ten: 1, 2, 3, 4, 5, 6, 7, 8, 9, 10. Take that time again to think. What do you think those two almost impossibly different people shared?

Since I am writing this, I have to tell you what I myself think. What this tiny little lady and this huge man share is the intensity of their capacity to examine and embrace the facts of the world they see about them. And then, furthermore, they both feel so strongly the richness and power of those facts that out of them they create a whole new vision of the world through their poetry, a world that otherwise would never have found its voice. Their vision now becomes a part of us who get to read them, and we are the richer for it.

You might find another correspondence between these two great American poets. Certainly they both placed their stamp on how poetry could be written, expanding the matter of it to include everything from the smallest bits of life (Miss Dickinson) to the largest ways of living (Mr. Whitman).

Walt Whitman, even, reflects much of what America is all about: confidence in ourselves as we march into the future. His confidence is a part of our hope post 9-11.

ANSWER THE QUESTION
AFTER (QUICKLY) READING
THE POEM:
DOES WHITMAN SEEM
CONFIDANT ABOUT HIMSELF
IN THE OPPORTUNITIES LIFE
PRESENTS?

From the "SONG OF THE OPEN ROAD"
Walt Whitman (1819 – 1892)

IS WHITMAN
MOST LIKE

A.) GEORGE
WASHINGTON

B.) EMILY
DICKINSON

C.) MR. MAGOO

D.) PAUL BUNYAN

E.) CASPAR, THE
FRIENDLY GHOST

Afoot and light-hearted I take to the open road,
Healthy, free, the world before me,
The long brown path before me leading where I choose.

Henceforth I ask not good-fortune, I myself am good-fortune,
Henceforth I whimper no more, postpone no more, need nothing,
Strong and content I travel the open road.

The earth, that is sufficient,
I do not want the constellations any nearer,
I know they are very well where they are,
I know they suffice for those who belong to them.

I inhale great draughts of space,
The east and the west are mine,
And the north and the south are mine.

I am larger, better than I thought,
I did not know I held so much goodness.

All seems beautiful to me,
I can repeat over to men and women, You have done
Such good to me I would do the same for you,
I will recruit myself and you as I go,
I will toss a new gladness and roughness among them,
Whoever denies me it shall not trouble me,
Whoever accepts me he or she shall be blessed and shall bless me.

Allons! Whoever you are come travel with me!
Traveling with me you find what never tires.

HOW MANY
TIMES
DOES THE
POET SAY "I"?

A.) 8 TIMES

B.) LOTS

C.) 19 TIMES

HOW MANY
TIMES DOES
A PERSON
HAVE TO
SAY "I"
BEFORE YOU
BEGIN TO THINK
THAT PERSON IS
PRETTY "FULL OF
HIMSELF"?

DOES IT
SEEM TO
MATTER TO
WHITMAN
WHICH
PATH
HE
TAKES
?

FRENCH FOR:
A.) LETS GO!
B.) STOP!
C.) LETS EAT!
D.) ALL ABOARD!

WHAT IS
THIS 'WHAT'?

Terms on p. 84

EDWARD LEAR (1812-1888)

When you get to Mr. Edward Lear, regarding whom there's nought to fear, you are, indeed, getting somewhere.

His, after all, is another kind of "poetry" altogether. Some people might not even want to call it "poetry," thinking that "poetry" should consist of serious, high-minded stuff, and that anything else is nothing more than "verse," "rhymes," "limericks," or just plain "doggerel." And lots of people, I dare say, tend to think that poetry is to words what opera is to music, so they get a little scared of it. What you are "scared of," you avoid, and so these people miss out on some great experiences in reading, and hearing, and seeing, that add a lot to one's perception and enjoyment of life.

OLD FOSS

A poem, each poem you read, is nothing more than its own little world, encapsulated, and handed to you on a silver platter (so to speak) by the poet, who has finely crafted through his words a vision, feeling, or thought that he or she possesses. The "game," of course, is to choose the very best words, and to place them in the very best order, and maybe to use a little meter, rhythm, or rhyme not only to engage us, but to enhance the feeling being expressed.

If you accept this definition, you will accept that for all of his whimsy, all of his absurdity, all of his ridiculosity, Edward Lear was a great poet. Aside from that, "how pleasant to know Mr. Lear"! And we know him, and admire and love him, for a variety of delightful reasons, long dead though he has now been.

Never mind that he was one of twenty children, which reminds me to compliment, and marvel at his Mom, and therefore, please, compliment all Moms everywhere. Early on he showed an aptitude for drawing, and indeed in his lifetime he was better known for his drawings and paintings than for his verse. When he was only 17 or 18, he created a wonderful series of paintings of parrots, which were so beautifully done that they gave him almost instantly a degree of minor fame. Really, he spent his life mostly as a painter, and having a rather adventuresome spirit, despite the fact that "his body is perfectly spherical," he traveled far and wide, drawing. He made drawings up the Nile, in Greece and Albania, and in Italy, where he finally settled with his cat, "Foss," whom he loved.

In the midst of his travels and drawings, Lear found time to put into words his risible, "runcible," rollicking perceptions of himself and life in general. He is all wild fancy and "nonsense." But don't forget: "fancy and nonsense" have a very important place in life, too. In fact, many say that there is no philosophy that benefits us more than having a good sense of humor. Lear, despite troubles in his life, despite even that he was afflicted from childhood by epileptic seizures (and there were no medicines to control them in those days) found the means to laugh at it all, and at himself to boot. His life and poetry are good lessons for us. So read again "The Owl and the Pussy-Cat."

Or maybe a favorite of mine, "The Pobble Who Has No Toes."

YES, INDEED !

HOW PLEASANT TO KNOW MR. LEAR
Edward Lear (1812-1888)

"STUFF", VOLUMES OF

"How pleasant to know Mr. Lear!"
Who has written such volumes of stuff!
Some think him ill-tempered and queer,
But a few think him pleasant enough.

His mind is concrete and fastidious,
His nose is remarkably big;
His visage is more or less hideous,
His beard it resembles a wig.

He has ears, and two eyes, and ten fingers;
Leastways if you reckon two thumbs;
Long ago he was one of the singers,
But now he is one of the dumbs.

He sits in a beautiful parlor,
With hundreds of books on the wall;
He drinks a great deal of Marsala,
But never gets tipsy at all.

He has many friends, lay men and clerical,
Old Foss is the name of his cat;
His body is perfectly spherical,
He weareth a runcible hat.

When he walks in waterproof white,
The children run after him so!
Calling out, "He's gone out in his night-
Gown, that crazy old Englishman, oh!"

He weeps by the side of the ocean,
He weeps on the top of the hill;
He purchases pancakes and lotion,
And chocolate shrimps from the mill.

He reads, but he cannot speak, Spanish,
He cannot abide ginger beer:
Ere the days of his pilgrimage vanish,
How pleasant to know Mr. Lear!

A KIND OF FORK WITH THREE... NO NOT TANGS, NOT TONGS... BUT TINES

I KNOW HIM

WILLIAM BUTLER YEATS (1865-1939)

Quite clearly, until now we have been dealing with— WHAT? The answer is that we have been looking at poets, American and English, and even Scottish, who wrote in the English language from about 1400 up into the nineteenth century. Of course, naturally, we have left out lots of poets, some who remain famous, and some who, although famous in their own day, are scarcely read at all now.

One other we cannot leave out. He wrote in English even though he did not consider himself English, and certainly not in the least "American." He came from where? Where else had English become a dominant language, even though the island itself rather violently resisted being a part of England and the British Empire? Ireland.

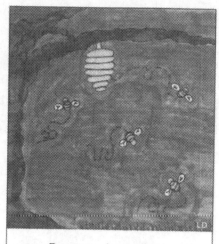

BEES IN A LOUD GLADE

The great poet of Ireland, most renowned among all the writers and poets of that green island, was William Butler Yeats. In his way, about a hundred years ago, Yeats, with the enthusiastic support of his friend and patron, Lady Gregory of Coole, almost alone created the very idea that Ireland was a place with its own wonderful culture and identity. Ever since the times of Queen Elizabeth I, and throughout the time Cromwell so ruthlessly subjugated it, Ireland's culture was suppressed by the English who lived there. The great talent of the Irish people for poetry, song, music, and dance had been forced to go "underground," overwhelmed by English attitudes and customs.

But by the end of the 1890s, a movement began which was aimed at revealing, resurrecting, and delighting in the ancient traditions held so dear by the Irish people.

Yeats was at the very forefront of this movement. In fact, one might say that he was the driving force behind the movement. It was his enthusiasm, inspiring other writers, poets, and playwrights, that carried high the banner of Irish Nationalism. The energy of his belief in the Irish cultural heritage resulted in a great flowering and love of all that is so wonderfully Irish. This rebirth is called "The Irish Renaissance."

Not only that, Yeats was one of the greatest of the "modern" poets. He was something of a mystic, that is a person who like the Irish themselves after all, love their leprechauns and fairies, and devotedly believe in the world of the spirit. In a letter to a friend defending magical practices, Yeats wrote that he was "a voice of the revolt of the soul against the intellect." Such a remark squarely places him in the tradition of the Romantic Poets, who rejected the concept that the reasoning of the mind alone was the only, or even the best, way to perceive and interpret the world we live in. Yeats thought that behind what we think we know, behind what we see, are ghosts and spirits that also direct our behavior, and these we can only know through our feelings. Feelings are to Yeats as important as, if not more so than, our intellect which thinks it knows more than it does.

Yeats's early poem about going to Innisfree, in the wilds of Ireland, is a beautiful expression of his longing to join his spirit to the mystery and magic of nature.

40

WHY NOT ANY ONE OR ALL OF THESE?

'PEACE' FROM WHAT?
A. HIS NEIGHBOR'S CHAIN SAW
B. LOUD TELEVISION
C. JET PLANES FLYING OVERHEAD
D. THE BUSY DEMANDS OF LIFE AMONG THE CROWDS

THE LAKE ISLE OF INNISFREE
William Butler Yeats (1865-1939)

RIGHT OFF THE BAT DO YOU GET AN IDEA THAT YEATS

A.) WANTS TO GO

B.) DOES NOT WANT TO GO

TO INNISFREE?

I will arise and go now, and go to Innisfree,
And a small cabin build there, of clay and wattles made;
Nine bean rows will I have there, a hive for the honey bee,
And live alone in the bee-loud glade.

WHAT ARE 'WATTLES'?
A. SOMETHING A DUCK DOES
B. A MIXTURE OF STRAW & MUD

And I shall have some peace there, for peace comes dropping slow,
Dropping from the veils of the morning to where the cricket sings;
There midnight's all a glimmer, and noon a purple glow,
And evening full of the linnet's wings.

DOES THIS SOUND LIKE
A. A HOPE
B. A DREAM
C. A PAINTING
D. ALL OF THAT ABOVE

I will arise and go now, for always night and day
I hear lake water lapping with low sounds by the shore;
While I stand on the roadway, or on the pavements gray,
I hear it in the deep heart's core.

NOW, IN ONE LINE, WRITE DOWN WHERE YOU MOST DREAM TO BE

ONE LINE → _____

AND SAVE THIS, TO LOOK AND SEE WHAT YOU WRITE 10, AND THEN 20, AND THEN 30 YEARS FROM NOW.

Terms on p. 86

EZRA POUND (1885-1972)

With Pound we arrive at the first of the poets whom we must call "modern." Yes, it is true that he began as a poet one whole hundred years ago. And yes, it is true that I who write this, I who flatter myself by wearing a Dr. Seuss's "cat in a hat" hat, was alive (to the best of my knowledge) during the last half of the lifetime of Ezra Pound. None of those points have much to do with what makes Pound "modern."

Pound is "modern" because he quite, let us say, invented a whole new direction for poetry, which it has pursued ever since. Pound came along at about the same time as Freud, who drastically changed the way we thought about the human mind. He came along at about the same time as Picasso,

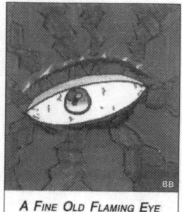

A FINE OLD FLAMING EYE

the great painter, who broke all the old "rules" of painting and showed us a new way of seeing the world. He came along at the same time as Einstein, who through mathematics was rearranging the ways that we had always thought about our whole universe.

All the old ways were being questioned, all the old rules broken. Poets began to use words differently, and for a different effect. Pound was foremost among them. And if he was hard to understand, everyone recognized that behind his words lay a new kind of power and depth and a beauty that almost burns. One wonders if in some strange way Pound was not himself burned up by his own genius. After all, "genius" does burn with an intense flame, and we are a little like moths, who can sometimes be consumed by their passion and ardor. In his poetry, Pound took us beyond all that had gone before, and left us a great legacy that we are still exploring. In doing so, he also got a little confused, mixing his poetry with politics, and finally, more or less, being declared "mad," by which I mean not angry but cuckoo-cuckoo.

Although born American, Pound lived most of his productive life in Europe, Italy in particular. He was in the forefront of a dynamic intellectual movement that was particularly active during the first twenty years of the twentieth century. He also became enamored with the dictatorship of Benito Mussolini, who had come to power in Italy in 1922. Mussolini's grandiose ideas, which Hitler himself adopted, appealed to Pound. Pound, sadly, thinking that "Musso" was the new wave of the future, supported his politics, and as a result was accused, when World War Two was over in 1945, of being a traitor. What to do with Pound? You could not quite *hang* one of the foremost poets of his age. And after all, he was "just a poet," without any real position of power in Italy.

Well, the courts and tribunals got out of it by declaring Pound "insane." After World War Two, he spent many of the remaining years of his life in St. Elizabeth's Hospital (for the mentally ill) just outside Washington, D.C.

Here is one of his early, "pretty" poems. He uses all sorts of old-fashioned words, from old-fashioned languages, to achieve an old-fashioned effect that is suddenly very modern. His great work, his long scheme of "Cantos," which quite goes on and on, and from which I have pulled out a fragment I have always loved, is mostly better saved for when you are over eighteen.

QUICKLY NOW WHAT IS
THIS NUMBER, WRITE IT
HERE IN ARABIC NUMERALS.
QUESTION: WHERE
DID OUR FORM
OF NUMBERS COME
FROM ?
A. ROME
B. GREECE
C. ARABIA
D. CHINA
—

From... **CANTO LXXXI**

Ezra Pound (1885-1972)

HOW IS AN
ANT, ANY
ANT,
THIS ?
CAN YOU THINK
OF ANTS AS
'CENTAURS' ?

What thou lov'st well remains,
            the rest is dross
What thou lov'st well shall not be reft from thee
What thou lov'st well is thy true heritage
Whose world, or mine or theirs
            Or is it of none?
First came the seen, then thus the palpable
    Elysium, though it were in the hall of hell,
What thou lov'st well is thy true heritage

The ant's a centaur in his dragon world.
Pull down thy vanity, it is not man
Made courage, or made order, or made grace,
      Pull down thy vanity, I say pull down.
Learn of the green world what can be thy place
In scaled invention or true artistry.
Pull down thy vanity,
           Paquin pull down!
The green casque has outdone your elegance...

But to have done instead of not doing
          this is not vanity
To have, with decency, knocked
That a Blunt should open
      To have gathered from the air a live tradition
or from a fine old eye the unconquered flame
This is not vanity.
    Here error is all in the not done,
all in the diffidence that faltered...

BIG TEST !
WHO
WILL LOOK
UP THESE
WORDS AND
TELL THEIR
MEANING ?

IS POUND
SAYING THAT
NATURE OR
PEOPLE ARE
THE STRONGEST ?

WHAT OTHER GROUP
OF POETS FIRST
BEGAN TO
THINK THE
SAME ?
A. PRE-SHAKESPERE,
LIKE CHAUCER
B.) CLASSICAL, LIKE
MILTON
C.) THE ROMANTICS

WHO CAN SAY
WHAT A 'BLUNT'
MIGHT BE ?
WOULD, WHATEVER IT
IS BE
SHARP OR DULL
SMART OR STUPID

FOR EXTRA CREDIT
WRITE A 15,000
WORD ESSAY
COMPARING THIS
'REMARK' TO THE
PHILOSOPHY
EXPRESSED IN THE
POEM BY
WHITMAN. FOR
A LITTLE CREDIT DOES
THIS STATEMENT SEEM
MORE TO AGREE
OR DISAGREE
WITH WHITMAN ?

Terms on p. 87

THOMAS STEARNS ELIOT (1888-1965)

Beyond Pound, it was T. S. Eliot who gave a poetic voice to our time. Indeed, one might assert that it was Eliot who, more than any poet, captured and defined the moods and misgivings of the twentieth century. Not only is he the greatest English poet of the century, he was also one of its greatest writers of critical essays about poetry and writers past and present. All of these are very serious works, but fascinating because of the power of the intellect and thought behind them. But if Eliot is almost overpowering, it is good to remember that beneath all that erudition was his ordinary love of cats. He wrote playful poems about them, which ultimately, long after Eliot's death, inspired the musical comedy "Cats," which you may have seen and heard.

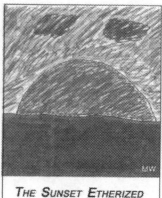

THE SUNSET ETHERIZED ON A TABLE

T. S. Eliot, although only three years younger than Pound, owed a great deal to the "older" man. Pound, it is said, "discovered" Eliot, and by way of his enthusiasm for Eliot's poems caused Eliot to change his mind about becoming a professor of philosophy, and instead commit himself to poetry and writing. Pound was always very generous in his recognition of talented poets to whom he gave his whole-hearted encouragement and support. For that reason Pound, above and beyond the greatness of his own poetry, played an important role in the way poetry evolved in the early twentieth century.

Pound's greatest discovery was Eliot. They met in 1915, when they were both living in England. By that time Eliot, who had graduated from Harvard a few years before, had written only a few poems, but one of them, "The Love Song of J. Alfred Prufrock," particularly excited Pound's admiration. He helped to get Eliot published, and then encouraged and even advised him in the writing of an even greater poem, "The Wasteland." These poems and others that followed in due course captured the despairing mood of the time, just before and after World War One.

That war was a great turning point. With it, everything people had formerly trusted, all the beliefs and hopes that had prevailed in the 19th century, were burst as though they had been struck by bombs. And they had been, truly. Millions of young men died in the trenches of World War One, and when it was all over nothing seemed as it had been before. Science and technology, as Tennyson himself had feared they might, had exploded all the old truths. People felt empty and bewildered and lost.

Eliot, who stayed in England to make it his home, gave words to these devastations of the spirit. The very title of "The Wasteland," which was published in 1922, says it all. But see also, in these opening lines of "The Love Song of J. Alfred Prufrock," how Eliot sets the stage for the gloomy and frightened images, images full of doubt and hesitation, that follow. For Prufrock, even "love" has become so dangerous that he dares not attempt it. He scarcely dares to "tie his tie." The people around him, meanwhile, go through the motions of life. The women, at their cocktail parties (which had just been invented then) "come and go, speaking of Michelangelo."

But it is just talk. Talk, talk, talk, without meaning, or passion, or even hope. Yes, Eliot caught the mood, and maybe even made some of it itself in this poem.

THE LOVE SONG OF J. ALFRED PRUFROCK
T. S. Eliot (1888 - 1965)

IS THIS A STRANGE WAY TO DESCRIBE A SUNSET ?

Let us go then, you and I.
When the sunset is spread out against the sky
Like a patient etherized upon a table:
Let us go through certain half-deserted streets.
The muttering retreats
Of restless nights in one-night cheap hotels
And sawdust restaurants with oyster shells:
Streets that follow like a tedious argument
Of insidious intent
To lead you to an overwhelming question...
Oh, do not ask, "What is it?"
Let us go and make our visit.

WHAT SORT OF WOMEN ? WHY MICHELANGELO ?

In the room the women come and go
Talking of Michelangelo

IS THIS MAN, THE J. ALFRED PRUFROCK OF ELIOT'S MIND MOST LIKE
A. WALT WHITMAN
B. CASPAR MILKTOAST
C. SCHWARZNEGGAR
D. SPIDERMAN

DOES PRUFROCK WORRY A LOT ABOUT WHAT PEOPLE THINK OF HIM ?

And indeed there will be time
To wonder, "Do I dare?" and, "Do I dare?"
Time to turn back and descend the stair.
With a bald spot in the middle of my hair—
(They will say: "How his hair is growing thin!")
My morning coat, my collar mounting firmly to the chin.
My necktie rich and modest, but asserted by a simple pin—
(They will say: "But how his arms and legs are thin!")
Do I dare
Disturb the universe?
In a minute there is time

JUDGING FROM THESE LINES WOULD YOU SAY PRUFROCK'S (OR ELIOT'S)

For decisions and revisions which a minute will reverse.
For I have known them all already, known them all:
Have known the evening, mornings, afternoons,
I have measured out my life with coffee spoons:
I know the voices dying with a dying fall
Beneath the music from a farther room.
So how should I presume?...

THIS IS A VERY FAMOUS LINE, YOU KNOW.

WAY OF DEALING WITH THE WORLD IS MOST LIKE WHICH ONE OF THE FOLLOWING POETS WE HAVE READ —
A. SHAKESPEARE
B. WHITMAN
C. EMILY DICKINSON
D. POE

45

THE WORLD WAR ONE POETS

World War Two was the biggest war, lasting from 1939 to 1945, but World War One, from 1914 to 1918, was more devastating. Many historians contend that World War Two was, in fact, simply a continuation of World War One.

Although Napoleon, more than a hundred years before the onset of World War One, had introduced the world to war on a great and ruthless scale, World War One came as a great shock from which we have not even yet recovered. For a hundred years there had been relative peace, and even though the American Civil War was fought on the Napoleonic scale and with fierce intensity, it did not destroy the idea that mankind could optimistically look forward to a bright and positive future.

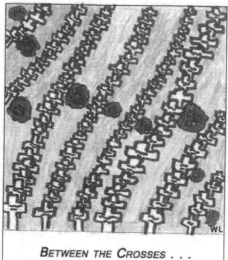

BETWEEN THE CROSSES . . .

World War One changed all that. As well, it depleted the world of the lives of millions of young men. Many of these, when the "whistle blew" and they "went over the top" to be mowed down by the newly invented machine gun, could doubtless have been brilliant leaders for their time: scientists, politicians, musicians, writers—and poets.

Such a massive loss of priceless lives left the world a lesser place. It also left the world embittered and angry, its hope replaced by doubt and cynicism. It was this, as we have seen, that T. S. Eliot so powerfully expressed in his poetry.

Doubts and misgivings, and anger too, were also expressed by a whole group of soldier-poets, who both as a group and as individuals cried out against the cruelty and insanity of a war that seemed to go on and on with little point except the killing. They did, all of them, do their duty, but their words rebelled. Their poems are beautifully written about an ugly topic, war. They created what remain the best words ever devised on the pity and pathos of war.

Many of the World War One poets, themselves, died. Rupert Brooke, already a poetic "superstar" before the war, at age 28. Julian Grenfell, age 27, socially renowned and "film-star" handsome. Charles Sorley, age 20, about whom Robert Graves, a poet and writer who did survive the war, said that despite his youth his loss was one of the greatest. Wilfred Owen, killed at age 25, but who left us some of that war's most powerful and frightening images. Isaac Rosenberg, age 28, whose poetry earned the highest respect from T. S. Eliot. Seigfried Sassoon, who did survive the war, and reap a just renown. But see how many died! They were younger, or scarcely older, than Keats, and their whole lives were taken away by machine gun bullets and high explosives.

Least and most of all was Lieutenant-Colonel John McCrae. "Least" because he wrote only one famous poem; but "most," because that poem was so very famous. It captured the waste and pity of the war in a way that none other did. His simple lines, written during the second battle of Ypres in 1915, were enormously admired. His words seemed more than any to speak for the dead. Then, by the end of 1918, McCrae himself had died and become one of them.

IN FLANDERS FIELD
John McCrae (1872-1918)

In Flanders Fields the poppies blow

Between the crosses, row on row,

That mark our place: and in the sky

The larks, still bravely singing, fly

Scarce heard amid the guns below.

We are the Dead. Short days ago

We lived, felt dawn, saw sunset glow,

Loved and were loved, and now we lie,

In Flanders fields.

Take up our quarrel with the foe:

To you from failing hands we throw

The torch: be yours to hold it high.

If ye break faith with us who die

We shall not sleep, though poppies grow

In Flanders fields.

DO YOU BELIEVE THAT WE, AND EVERY GENERATION, MUST FOLLOW THE LIGHT, 'HOLD HIGH THE TORCH, OF WHAT WE BELIEVE IN'?

Terms on p. 89

DON MARQUIS (1878-1937)

Like music, poetry sings many different songs, and in as many different ways as there are personalities who write poems. You are yourself a poet, scarcely knowing it. The words you speak in your response to the world are, after all, chosen by no one but you. The poet is simply a person who enjoys the choosing of words, serious or playful, and arranging them in a way that creates a word-picture of what is seen and felt. Kids are famously good at poetry because their eyes see the world so freshly.

1927   1933   1935

MARQUIS'S BOOKS

They are not afraid to put together sometimes surprising and brilliant combinations of words that grown-ups, out of long stiffened habits of seeing and saying more or less the same things over and over, forget they can do.

In other words, the poetry is there. It is in you. Its style and content run a whole range all the way from the fanciful word-play of Edward Lear right up to that rather lonely pinnacle where great poetic intellects, such as Milton and T. S. Eliot sit composing their mighty poems.

Now, one cannot say that the "poems" of Don Marquis are mighty in that sense. In fact some might say that what he wrote were not "poems" at all. But I think they are, and indeed rather wonderfully "are." They may not be on the great scale of poetry written from the high heights of the intellect of T. S. Eliot or John Milton. They may in fact be even "lower" than the whimsical verses of Edward Lear. But they wonderfully say something in a delightful way.

After all, when was there ever a poet before who wrote so engagingly about a stray cat in a big city and her friend, a cockroach, who wrote poetry himself? And between these two, and the dialogues they have with one another, do we not see life through a different "glass" and learn some wonderful lessons about it? We do for sure.

Marquis was a reporter for a large New York paper. He lived in the big, brash, and bawdy world of the 1920s, a world trying to forget the terrible events of World War One, a world famous for its new freedoms, new money, big parties, fast cars, flappers and "Prohibition," that law that no one paid much attention to, but which prohibited the sale of alcoholic beverages. He drew out of this world, which could be rather tough, a wonderful series of sketches, starring Archie, the roach, and his friend Mehitabel, the cat. Everyone loved these two personalities, who despite the worst circumstances (who, after all, wants to be a roach?) always rose with good humor above their trials. As Mehitabel said, when her litter of kitten all drowned in the garbage can where they were living, "Always a lady, Archie, always a lady. There's a dance in the old girl yet."

Well, some might say it "ain't poetry." But I think otherwise. After the terrible tragedies of World War One, Archie and Mehitabel gave our hopes a way out of despair. Archie, the roach, aspired to be Shakespeare. These little stories, with their wry but cheerful message, seem to me to be quite like Chaucer's tales. In fact, I can very clearly see Mehitabel and Archie as part of the company of those pilgrims on their way to Canterbury. If there is a "Knight's Tale," why not a cat's—or even a cockroach's?

from "Archy and Mehitabel"
Don Marquis (1878-1937)

mehitabel the cat claims that
she has a human soul
also and has transmigrated
from body to body and it
may be so boss you
remember i told you she accused
herself of being cleopatra once...

i had some romantic
lives and some elegant times i
have seen better days archy but
whats the use of kicking kid its
all in the game like a gentleman
friend of mine used to say
toujours gai kid toujours gai he
was an elegant cat he used
to be a poet himself and he made up
some elegant poetry about me and him
lets hear it i said and
mehitabel recited
persian pussy from over the sea
demure and lazy and smug and fat
none of your ribbons and bells for me
ours is the zest of the alley cat
over the roofs from flat to flat
we prance with capers corybantic
what though a boost should break a slat
mehitabel us for the life romantic
we would rather be rowdy and gaunt and free
and dine on a diet of roach and rat
roach i said what do you
mean roach interrupting mehitabel
yes roach she said thats the
way my boy friend made it up
i climbed in amongst the typewriter
keys for she had an excited
look in her eyes go on mehitabel i
said feeling safer and she
resumed her elocution
we would rather be rowdy and gaunt and free
and dine on a diet of roach and rat
than slaves to a tame society
ours is the zest of the alley cat
fish heads freedom a frozen sprat
dug from the gutter with digits frantic
is better than bores and a fireside mat
mehitabel us for the life romantic
when the pendant moon in the leafless tree
clings and sways like a golden bat
i sing its light and my love for thee
ours is the zest of the alley cat
missiles around us fall rat a tat tat
but our shadows leap in a ribald antic
as over the fences the world cries scat
mehitabel us for the life romantic

CAN A SCRUFFY ALLEY CAT REALLY BELIEVE SHE WAS ONCE CLEOPATRA?

WHY NOT?

FRENCH FOR 'ALWAYS MERRY', 'ALWAYS GAY'

WOULD THIS CAT BE A BETTER COMPANION FOR
A. EMILY DICKINSON
B. WALT WHITMAN

WHAT IS ARCHY AFRAID MEHITABEL MIGHT DO TO HIM, GOOD FRIEND THOUGH SHE IS?

WHAT PLAY, MADE INTO A FILM BASED ON POEMS BY T.S. ELIOT, HAS CHARACTERS IN IT WHO SOUND LIKE THIS?
A.) THE SOUND OF MUSIC
B.) LES MISERABLES
C.) CATS
D.) PETER PAN

ARCHY IS THE COCKROACH WHO ASPIRED TO BE POET, AND WROTE THESE POEMS.

MEHITABEL IS HIS FRIEND, THE ALLEY CAT, ABOUT WHOM ARCHY OFTEN WRITES.

e e cummings (1894-1962)

Agree with me, please, that it is by now perfectly clear that there are many ways and forms of writing poetry. We have seen the rigid mannerisms imposed on it so brilliantly by Pope, and his demand that it should be written in "heroic couplets." We have seen how Archie, the roach, aspired to becoming a *vers libre* (free verse) poet, which demands neither rhyme nor meter. We have seen how Shakespeare, almost at the very beginning, was a genius at all these forms, and felt free to use any he chose for his poetic and dramatic purposes.

AGAINST THE MOON'S FACE

We have also seen that during World War One the whole world felt fractured by its tragedy of death and loss. Artists described as "Cubists" and "Dadaists" started depicting the world in agonized bits and broken splashes. Composers of music began to explore strange sounds that seemed odd, and even harsh in their dissonances. Writers produced works whose language reflected the dark, broken fragments that lie swirling beneath the surface of the mind, rather like those strange fish that lie in the deepest depths of the oceans. Poets, of course, were caught up in this new vision of the world, some in such an extreme way that they are scarcely comprehensible at all. Edward Estlin Cummings, although part of that movement, happily remains not only understandable, but delightful to the mind and ear.

cummings's poems often come in what seem fractured bits and pieces, but each some-how gathers itself up at the end to leave us with a vivid image, everything coming suddenly together with, more often than not, a hopeful, even happy, possibility.

Why did he not use capital letters? And why, sometimes, do the visual shapes of his poems not quite look as we think a poem should? Why did he call his "sonnets" "sonnets" when they did not have fourteen lines, and did not at all conform to the accepted rhyme scheme and meter of what we had earlier scrupulously defined as "sonnets"? Who could fully say, even cummings? But let us guess that he did so because he was, after all, seeing and seeking the new forms for things and feelings that so gripped the "new" world in the aftermath of World War One. He avoided the use of capital letters in his poems, and signed his name to them, "e e cummings," without any capitals. Of course, merely that simple fact alone caught everyone's eye, and that may be even a part of the reason he did it. But, more deeply, it was a way of stating that people, and poems too, were now different from what we had once grown used to expecting. By not using the capitals when you write a name, does it imply that people, in the midst of nature and in the aftermath of so much war, seem "smaller"? What do you think?

e e cummings, after graduating from Harvard, drove an ambulance in World War One. He was held prisoner for a while during and just after the war, and wrote an interesting book called *The Enormous Room* about the experience. After the war he settled down in Greenwich Village in New York City, an area that appealed then and now to artists. He wrote many poems, and made a big name for himself. This one, SONNET: V, shows what he thought a sonnet could be like. The image in the last two lines, for me has always stood for Hope. It comes so suddenly–but it is there!

HOW MANY LINES SHOULD A "SONNET" HAVE?

A. 14
B. 9
C. 7
D. 1,345

HOW MANY LINES DOES THIS "SONNET" HAVE?

BUT! WAIT. COULD YOU, IF YOU WANTED, (BUT WHO WOULD 'WANT'?) REARRANGE A FEW OF THESE LINES TO MAKE IT A PROPER, FORMAL 'SONNET'? WHAT IS CUMMINGS TELL US ABOUT HIS IDEAS OF 'PROPER FORM'?

WHY DID CUMMINGS NOT USE CAPITALS IN HIS NAME? WHO KNOWS?

SONNET : V

e e cummings (1894 – 1962)

a wind has blown the rain away and blown
the sky away and all the leaves away,
and the trees stand. I think i too have known
        Autumn too long.

            (and what have you to say,
wind wind wind—did you love somebody
and have you the petal of somewhere in your heart
pinched from dumb summer?
            O crazy daddy
of death dance cruelly for us and start

the last leaf whirling in the final brain
of air!) Let us as we have seen see
doom's integration......................a wind has blown the rain

away and leaves and the sky and the
trees stand:
        the trees stand. The tree's
suddenly wait against the moon's face.

WHEN DID ROBERT FROST DIE?

A. 1961
B.) 1962
C.) 1963

DOES THIS POEM SEEM TO YOU TO END
A. HOPEFULLY
B. NOT HOPEFULLY
C. DOWNRIGHT HOPELESSLY

WHAT MAKES IT SEEM SO?

A. THE WIND
B.) THE CRAZY DADDY
C.) TREES
D) THE MOON

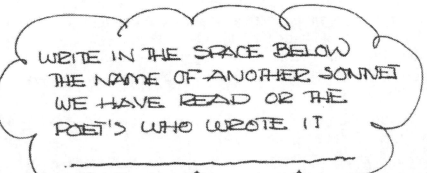

WRITE IN THE SPACE BELOW THE NAME OF ANOTHER SONNET WE HAVE READ OR THE POET'S WHO WROTE IT

_____

51

ROBERT FROST (1874-1963)

Who does not know Robert Frost? He has become a part of the American idea and tradition, rather like Whitman. And besides, his poems LOOK like poems, and SOUND like poems. In a world, both poetic and otherwise, that whirls so about us, ever shifting and changing in its currents, Frost was and remains something of a poetic anchor. He can be relied on to look both wisely and deeply into rather homely, earthy subjects that we all can share. He seems familiar. He takes us with him to places down a road that we can recognize. Through the beauty of his words he makes each poetic "trip" a small adventure that somehow, almost miraculously, gets into one's own self, and is never forgotten.

RIGHT? LEFT?

A road. A tree. A wall. Snow falling. These are the commonplace ingredients of his poetry. Around these things Frost weaves his magic spell, often leaving us with a thoughtful question that we ponder, and so grow a bit wiser in our understanding. Who is not grateful to Frost? The sound and form of his poetry demand our trust. We can put our faith in Frost. In an uncertain world, he leads us back to the basic facts of life, while at the same time showing us the wonder and mystery that reside in simple things. A road. A tree. A wall. Snow.

Frost went to England, too, just about the same time as Pound and Eliot. He met other poets and writers. But he was not tempted by all the bold new styles that were, sometimes quite self-consciously, attempting to break with the past, or simply shock. He was, after all, a New Englander. In his blood were generations of his forefathers who had lived and wrested a living out of that hard, rocky soil. He did not stay long in England, even though he was admired and in fact achieved his first fame there. He longed for his New Hampshire roots. He came home, bought a farm, looked about him, and then, for years, made poetry of what he saw.

He lived a long life. As he lived it, his poetry more and more captivated not just those who read him, but our whole nation. Even people who never read poetry at all knew of Robert Frost. He and his poems became almost as one, and both were revered. His poetry, and he the man, came to embody the best of America: the simplicity, the straightforwardness, the honesty, the honor of hard work and play. Most of all, his poetry reflects a questing search for what is right, even if Frost himself cannot give us the answer. No one can. It is the search, thoughtful and probing, that matters, and that leads our hopes toward the creation of a better world.

In his closeness to nature and his deep respect for what nature can teach us, Frost was for us in America what Wordsworth had been for England a hundred years earlier. It is why President Kennedy made Frost America's "Poet Laureate," and had him come, in the dignity of his advanced age, to the White House, to give a public reading. Oh, everyone cheered, and all America was proud.

Read this poem, "The Road Not Taken." Unlike Whitman (do you remember?) does it matter to Frost what road he takes? Does it matter to you?

CAN YOU THINK WAY
A 'ROAD NOT TAKEN'
MIGHT BE AS
IMPORTANT AS 'A
ROAD TAKEN'?

THE ROAD NOT TAKEN
Robert Frost (1875 – 1963)

WHO 'TOOK
TO THE
OPEN
ROAD' AND
DID NOT
CARE
WHICH HE
TOOK?

Two roads diverged in a yellow wood.
And sorry I could not travel both
And be one traveler, long I stood
And looked down one as far as I could
To where it bent in the undergrowth:

Then took the other, as just as fair,
And having perhaps the better claim,
Because it was grassy and wanted wear;
Though as for that the passing there
Had worn them really about the same.

And both that morning equally lay
In leaves no step had trodden black.
Oh, I kept the first for another day!
Yet knowing how way leads on to way,
I doubted if I should ever come back.

I shall be telling this with a sigh
Somewhere ages and ages hence:
Two roads diverged in a road, and I—
I took the one less traveled by,
And that has made all the difference.

A. EMILY DICKINSON
B. MILTON
C.) KEATS
D.) WHITMAN

IN MAKING
THE CHOICE
REGARDING
WHICH ROAD
TO TAKE,
DOES FROST
FIND THE
DECISION
A. IMPOSSIBLE
B.) VERY HARD
C.) SOMETHING
TO CONSIDER
D.) EASY

WHY WOULD
HE DOUBT IF
HE WOULD EVER
'COME BACK'?

CONSIDER:
CAN YOU
COME BACK
TO THE
5TH, 6TH, OR
7TH GRADE?

DOES THE POET LIKE TO
A. DO LIKE EVERYONE ELSE
B. TRY SOMETHING DIFFERENT
C. ALWAYS GIVE IN TO
'PEER PRESSURE'

Terms on p. 91

WALLACE STEVENS (1879-1955)

Stevens, too, was a New Englander, but how very different seems the poetic world he creates compared to that of Robert Frost. They were different as people, too. Frost was a man of the land, who lived on his farm in New Hampshire. Stevens lived in the rather large city of Hartford, Connecticut, and was (rare for a poet!) a "business-man" who became the Vice-President of a large, nationally known insurance company. Frost drew his poetry from simple things that he saw about him. Stevens created a rather exotic poetical world, of course out of his own experience, but often arising out of what I am going to call (a bit "poetically"!) the rich tapestry of his own mind and imagination. Perhaps poetry was his "escape" from the business of "Business."

CHIEF IF YOU CAN IN
CAFTAN OF TAN

Now, let's face it! Stevens is "hard." He is "hard," for the same reason that Eliot and Pound are "hard," because they use words and images that are unfamiliar to our ordinary ways of speaking. Unlike Frost, who wrote about everyday things using everyday words, these poets made use of a less familiar vocabulary, and made juxtapositions of words to create a different magic. Stevens loved the relationships between words themselves, the ways they sounded together, the ways they rolled off the tongue. Sometimes, even without our understanding quite what is meant, the words themselves please us by their sound alone. Stevens may be hard to understand for a sixth grader, even for a seventh or eighth, but he haunts you nonetheless, and as you get older, you will enjoy reading him more and more. So there is no better time to know something of him than right now.

Poetry, for Stevens, was an act of the mind discovering itself, and through that discovery giving meaning to what we perceive, to what confronts us. Every time we think about anything at all, we discover a little something more of ourselves. What we see becomes finally what we think about what we see. There is a poem Stevens wrote about the sea, called "The Idea of Order at Key West," in which a girl walks by the ocean. She and the sea become one because, Stevens tells us, the sea is what the girl thinks, or as he put it "sings," about the sea: "And when she sang, the sea, whatever self it had, became the self that was her song, for she was the maker." Have you ever thought what an ocean could be if there was no eye to see it, and no mind to think about it?

Stevens thinks deeply on this point. Even when his words seem strung together simply for the fun of the sounds he creates, behind that "fun" there is serious purpose. Consider his little poem, "Bantams in Pine-Woods." I have long enjoyed it. I have always seen Chieftain Iffucan as a great "Fat! Fat! Fat! Fat!" blob of a Pooh-bah, full of himself as a "ten foot poet," and rather a bully. Even if we think ourselves mere "inchlings," our minds can make us larger and greater, so that we can quite "bristle in these pines," and fear not the threats and "hoos" of "portly (Fat!) Azcan," despite "his caftan of tan and henna hackles." We will make him "halt!" and will point our "Appalachian tangs" at him! We are, after all, who we are!

It is through "the poem of the mind," Stevens says, that we find and make "what will suffice."

TELL ME, IF YOU CAN,
CAN I CAN AS
WELL AS YOU CAN 'CAN'?

DOES THIS
POEM SUGGEST
TO YOU THAT
WE, OURSELVES,
ARE THE CREATORS
OF OUR WORLDS?

Bantams in Pine-Woods
Wallace Stevens (1879-1955)

Chieftain Iffucan of Azcan in caftan
Of tan with henna heckles, halt!

Damned universal cock, as if the sun
Was blackamoor to bear your blazing tail.

Fat! Fat! Fat! Fat! I am the personal.
Your world is you. I am my world.

You ten-foot poet among inchlings. Fat!
Begone! An inchling bristles in these pines,

Bristles, and points their Appalachian tangs,
And fears not portly Azcan nor his hoos.

A FIERCE LITTLE FELLOW
IN FULL BRISTLE

IS THIS
'INCHLING'
PRETTY PROUD
AND WILLING
TO DEFEND HIS
'PINES'?

↓

YES ——
NO ——
MAYBE ——

↓

DO YOU
KNOW ANY
'INCHLINGS'?

↓

ARE YOU ONE?

THAT
IS TO
SAY, DON'T YOU THINK,
THAT NONE OF US, AND,
CERTAINLY NO 'INCHLING',
NEED BE AFRAID OF
EVERY 'BOO', OR 'HOO', OR
EVEN 'BOO-HOO'!

DO YOU
KNOW ANY
'FOOTLINGS'?
(HA-HA)

55

CONRAD AIKEN (1889-1973)

There was a time, I think I can say, when Conrad Aiken was one of my favorite poets. He has not been everyone's.

But to me his poems were what poems should be. He did not seem to mystify for the sake of mystification. His poems possessed a nice balance between thought and feeling, and how both interact with the world surrounding us, which is, after all, magical. Although he was in fact criticized for his preoccupation with the musical quality of how he arranged the words of his poems, with their rhythms up and down, I enjoy this quality. His poems, as he himself said, do not so much "arouse" an emotion, but "employ" it with "the same cool detachment with which a composer employs notes or chords."[1] There is a fluid, watery, mellifluous quality to his work that has been

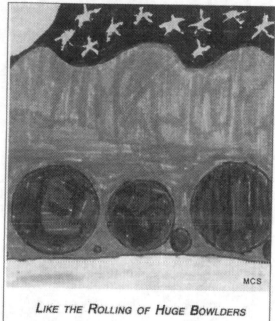

LIKE THE ROLLING OF HUGE BOWLDERS

compared to the music of Debussy. His poems are to be heard aloud, with your eyes half closed, not just to be seen and read silently.

Along with the music of his words, he wrote of things within my understanding, but surrounded them with enchantment, and cast a certain spell that showed me another side, another plane, to the "reality" my own eyes saw. Without bewildering me, he challenged both my mind and my imagination. There is a sort of "fairy-tale" quality to his work that I relished, and the "music" of his words led me on.

I think he liked boats, too.

Although born in Savannah, Georgia, Aiken was raised by an Aunt in Massachusetts after the tragic death of both his parents when he was 11 years old. He attended Harvard, shared a class with T. S. Eliot, and was elected the class poet for his graduating year in 1912. He spent a lot of time in England during the 1920s, along with many of the other poets we have read, and was responsible for introducing many American poets to the English. One of these was Emily Dickinson, whose "discovery" and popularity were the result of Aiken's editing and publishing a volume of her work in 1924. Unlike any of the other poets we have studied, except for Edgar Allen Poe, Aiken also wrote short stories, equally lyrical (except they were in prose) and with the same atmosphere of haunting enchantment.

During an early period of his life, he went back and forth between the United States and England, finally settling in Massachusetts by the cold and misty sea. There he lived in a house from which he could look out and see the masts of sailboats, rhythmically swaying in the swell, and could hear the rhythm of the waves on the rocky shore. In winters he would go back to Savannah, where he lived in the house where he had grown up as a child. Wherever he was, he "guessed" the presence of angels, and strove not to be blind.

OF COURSE YOU COULD LOOK IT UP IN THE DICTIONARY BUT I AM GOING TO TELL YOU (HAVING LOOKED IT UP MYSELF THAT 'AVATAR' IS A HINDU WORD DERIVED FROM SANSRIT THAT DESCRIBES THE FACT OF A GOD COMING TO EARTH IN PHYSICAL FORM.

Miracles
Conrad Aiken (1889-1973)

DO 'BOWLDERS' STRIKING TOGETHER MAKE A BIGGER SOUND THAN 'BOULDERS'?

HAVE YOU EVER HAD THOUGHTS THAT FLIT THROUGH YOUR BRAIN LIKE A BAT?

Twilight is spacious, near things in it seem far,
And distant things seem near.
Now in the green west hangs a yellow star,
And now across old waters you may hear
The profound gloom of bells among still trees,
Like a rolling of huge bowlders beneath seas.

HERE, NOW, IS AN INTERESTING WORD

Silent as thought in evening contemplation
Weaves the bat under the gathering stars.
Silent as dew, we seek new incarnation,
Meditate new avatars.
In a clear dusk like this
Mary climbed up the hill to seek her son,
To lower him down from the cross, and kiss
The mauve wounds, every one.

WHAT ARE THEY?

WHAT ARE THEY DOING TO MAKE THE BURDEN LIGHTER?

Men with wings
In the dusk walked softly after her.
She did not see them, but may have felt
The winnowed air around her stir;
She did not see them, but may have known
Why her son's body was light as a little stone.
She may have guessed that other hands were there
Moving the watchful air.

AS WHEN YOU LET THE WIND SEPARATE GRAIN FROM CHAFF OR IF YOU HAD A HANDFUL OF MARBLES MIXED WITH BITS OF TISSUE PAPER, AND THREW THE LOT INTO THE BREEZY AIR, WHAT WOULD BLOW AWAY AND WHAT WOULD FALL TO YOUR FEET, 'WINNOWED'

Now, unless persuaded by searching music
Which suddenly opens the portals of the mind,
We guess no angels,
And are contented to be blind.
Let us blow silver horns in the twilight,
And lift our hearts to the yellow star in the green,
To find perhaps, if, while the dew is rising,
Clear things may not be seen.

THESE LINES, AFTER 'SILENT UPON A PEAK IN DARIEN', (WHO WROTE THAT?) ARE MY THIRD FAVORITE LINES FROM THIS COURSE

57

OGDEN NASH (1902-1971)

Now remember, this "course" is not supposed to be tiresome and tedious. It is supposed to be, vaguely, kind of, sort of, sometimes, interesting and maybe even fun. Some poets, of course, are more serious than others, and they get a lot of attention because they put their serious thoughts about life in a poetically fascinating way that we get to work at figuring out, almost like a puzzle.

Then there is Edward Lear, who, as we have seen, simply has fun with verse.

LITTLE? LOTTLE?

Also there is Ogden Nash. He is as wonderfully ridiculous with words as Lear, whom he admired, naturally. As a matter of fact, he even out-Leared Lear. As whimsical and witty as Lear was, and as preposterous, outrageous, ridiculous, and nonsensical as Lear's limericks could be, Ogden Nash surpassed everyone in his invention of the most absurd and delightfully laughable rhythms and rhymes. He thought nothing of inventing a word when he needed it, just to rhyme it with another, but always his "inventions" are carried off with such style, such great panache (there is a word for you!) that once you have read them they seem perfect in their place. In a way that is what poetry is about. . You may be as serious as Milton, or as light-hearted as Nash, but the point is to find, even to invent, the best combination of words that will express your thought and feeling.

Nash grew up near New York City. His great-great-grandfather was the Governor of North Carolina, and his brother was a general in the Revolutionary War, whose name was given to what was then a frontier village. We now know that town as Nashville, Tennessee. (This, by the way, is an excellent bit of trivia for you to remember.) After his youthful youth, Nash went for one year to Harvard, class of 1924, and entered the business of selling bonds. He sold only one, he said, and that was to his godmother. Then, in 1930, he wrote one of his verses, which he threw in the wastebasket. He thought better of it, fished it out, and sent it to "The New Yorker," a magazine both then and now famous for its literary quality. He was almost immediately recognized as a unique talent, and in 1932 he joined the editorial staff of that magazine.

Thereafter all sorts of poems and books poured from his prolific pen. He was called "God's gift to the United States" by "The Atlantic Monthly," another literary publication ordinarily very serious in its observations. Archibald MacLeish, also a great poet, critic, and panjandrum, said that Nash had "altered the sensibility of his time." As for Nash himself, he merely said, "my field is the minor idiocies of humanity." One of his collections of poems, such collections sometimes being called "Treasuries," was renamed by some witty critic "The Golden Trashery of Ogden Nashery."

If there is a poet almost impossible not to like, it is Nash. He is one of the most quoted of poets because he stays so neatly on the tip of your tongue despite his plays on words and absurd rhymes, or maybe because of them. In any case, Nash became and still remains a great American fixture. He also tells us that humor can see one through, and, at that, maybe better than even all your most serious poets lined up in their robes in a row.

Selected fauna and a catsup bottle
Ogden Nash (1902-1971)

NOTHING NEED BE SAID ABOUT ANY OF THESE: SIMPLY READ THEM

The Fly
The Lord in his wisdom made the fly,
And then forgot to tell us why

The Cow *HA-HA*
The cow is of the bovine ilk,
One end is moo, the other milk.

The Jellyfish
Who wants my jellyfish?
I'm not sellyfish.

The Ant
The ant has made himself illustrious
Through constant industry industrious.
So what?
Would you be calm and placid,
If you were full of formic acid?

The Centipede
I objurgate the centipede,
A bug we do not really need.
At sleepy-time he beats a path
Straight to the bedroom or the bath.
You always wallop where he's not,
Or, if he is, he makes a spot.

The firefly
The firefly's flame is something for which science has no name
I can think of nothing eerier
Than flying around with an unidentified glow on a
Person's posterior.

The Ostrich
The ostrich roams the great Sahara.
Its mouth is wide, its neck is narra.
It has such long and lofty legs,
I'm glad it sits to lay its eggs.

The Shrimp
A shrimp who sought his lady shrimp
Could catch no glimpse
Not even a glimp.
At times, translucence
Is rather a nuisance

The Abominable Snowman
I've never seen an abominable snowman,
I'm hoping not to see one,
I'm also hoping, if I do,
That it will be a wee one.

The Octopus
Tell me, O Octopus, I begs
Is those things arms, or is they legs?
I marvel at thee, Octopus;
If I were thou, I'd call me Us.

The Catsup Bottle *HA!*
First a little
Then a lottle } *MY 4TH FAVORITE LINES IN THIS COURSE*

The Camel
The camel has a single hump;
The dromedary, two;
Or else the other way around,
I'm never sure. Are you?

The Duck
Behold the duck
It does not cluck,
A cluck it lacks.
It quacks.
It is special fond
Of a puddle or a pond.
When it dines or sups, } *HA-HA-HA !*
It bottoms ups.

Eels
I don't mind eels
Except as meals
And the way they
feels.

The Hippopotamus
Behold the hippopotamus!
We laugh at how he looks at us,
And yet in moments dank and grim
I wonder how we look to him.
Peace, peace, thou hippopotamus!
We really look all right to us,
As you no doubt delight the eye
Of other hippopotami.

STEPHEN SPENDER (1909-1995)

Having arrived at the "modern" poets, by which I mean those who have written in our own time, I find selection more and more difficult. Just think of all the wonderful words that have been written by just good, or excellent, or even brilliant people that you and I will never read. Think of the writers, and poets in particular, whose names might have been known to all in the time of Dryden or Gray, but whose works we do not read today at all. Fashions come and go, and the words of one generation may not appeal to the next. Sometimes, as with Emily Dickinson for example, or Keats, the words come "before their time," and are not "discovered" until long after the poet is dead.

FÊTED BY . . .

The decade of the 1930s was a rich time poetically. Poetical giants such as Eliot, Pound, and Yeats, still alive and writing, had redefined the course of poetry. The bitterness left after the horrors of World War One was compounded by the great world-wide economic depression. The rise of the totalitarian dictatorships of Hitler, Mussolini, and Stalin seemed an ominous portent for the world, and did lead finally in 1939 to the outbreak of World War Two.

In this period, numerous poets reflected deep concern and anxiety over all of these issues. A poet named W. H. Auden became, perhaps, the major voice expressive of these times. Another "voice" was that of Stephen Spender. Together with Auden and other English poets, many of whom had gone "up to" Oxford at about the same time in the 1920s, Spender was deeply concerned by the dark forces that seemed to be gripping the world. The power of mechanical things, airplanes, trains, power plants ("the gasworks") both repelled and fascinated him. He could write of these things, so foreign to the usual habit of poetry, which once upon a time had devoted itself to the prettier images of nightingales, swans, larks, clouds, sunsets, and all the rest. Some people felt that he put too much "politics" into his poems, too, as though poetry should be "above" such a dirty subject.

Perhaps Spender's most famous poem, however, is none of that. Yes, it mentions "traffic" (NOT a very "poetic" topic!) but also "blossoms," "high fields," "waving grass," and "clouds," all highly acceptable to the traditions of poetic speech. This poem, "I Think Continually of Those…" reminds one more of Keats in some ways than of Spender's own other poems. In it he permits himself to express sentiments that in some of his other poems he seems almost to want to hide. The "thirties" was a tough time, in many ways a despairing time, and Spender, despite the beauty of his turns of phrase, was a part of it. But in this poem he allows beauty, admiration, and deeply felt sentiment to speak above and beyond his immediate anxiety.

The choice is hard. I suppose I should have chosen Auden over Spender. But this is a poem I have loved. I read it at my Mother's funeral. I once heard Spender himself read it aloud, in 1970, when he was distinguished in his years. I think of it often. When I see someone I admire, who is overcoming a difficult circumstance with courage, phrases from this poem spring to my mind. It must therefore be included here, for you, too, to remember, and to remind you where courage comes from..

I Think Continually of Those...
(Stephen Spender, 1909-1995)

I think continually of those who were truly great.
Who, from the womb, remembered the soul's history
Through corridors of light where the hours are suns,
Endless and singing. Whose lovely ambition
Was that their lips, still touched with fire,
Should tell of the spirit clothed from head to foot in song.
And who hoarded from the spring branches
The desires falling across their bodies like blossoms.

What is precious is never to forget
The delight of the blood drawn from ageless springs
Breaking through rocks in worlds before our earth;
Never to deny its pleasure in the simple morning light,
Nor its grave evening demand for love;
Never to allow gradually the traffic to smother
With noise and fog the flowering of the spirit.

Near the snow, near the sun, in the highest fields
See how these names are fêted by the waving grass,
And by the streamers of white cloud,
And whispers of wind in the listening sky:
The names of those who in their lives fought for life,
Who wore at their hearts the fire's center.
Born of the sun they traveled a short while towards the sun,
And left the vivid air signed with their honor.

HERE
↓
IS WHERE WE CAME FROM
↓

HERE
IS WHAT WE MUST REMEMBER AND HOLD CLOSE
↓

AND HERE IS THE HONOR WE GAIN BY DOING SO.

THESE ARE MY SECOND FAVORITE LINES IN THIS COURSE.

DO YOU KNOW ANYONE THEY COULD HAVE BEEN WRITTEN ABOUT?

61

THE STEPS UP

Langston Hughes (1902-1967)

Some things are easy to calculate. Two plus two makes four.

But how do you calculate the spirit? How do you calculate courage? How do you add up grit, determination, hope, and hard work?

The beating heart, which might after all average 75 beats a minute, which for 75 years adds up to a whooping 2,956,500,000 (do the math, and as a real test without a calculator) beats. This is, for sure a "Wow!" But who can say what, with each of those beats, the "heart", by which I mean the "poetic heart", or spirit, was feeling, suffering, wishing, praying, or singing? In between the numbers lies the reality and the mystery.

It is this reality that poetry explores.

It is this reality that black poets, torn from their African roots, have for generations sought to understand. They have done do with a unique and special voice, and by all manner of means: Through their music, which has given the entire world a fresh means of listening to the soul within us; through their faith and hope, which has risen above the harshest circumstances of slavery; through their hard work, which created so much of our world; and not to leave out the good humor with which they did it, and without which the world would be a sad and sorry place.

One cannot add these notions up.

There is no telling how far back brilliant rhythms, and poignant words, drawing on ancient memories, have been seated at the very heart of the black-African spirit. And yes, they brought with them from Africa all of this, which in our own colonial times had profound local effect on our culture. It was only, however, after the Civil War, and emancipation, freeing all the slaves, that the voice of African-Americans could be truly expressed. And even then it was hard. But gradually, more and more, American blacks found that voice until, with growing sound throughout the 20th century, it became a powerful force within our nation and the world.

And there were poets who helped it to become so. Langston Hughes was one.

From the 1920s until his death from cancer in 1967 he was, in fact, the great poetic voice, the *poet laureate,* of his people. At a time when other black poets were attempting to write poems within the tradition of American and English poetry, as we have studied it, Langston Hughes gave powerful expression to his own culture. In a famous essay of his published in 1926, he wrote that "we younger Negro artists now intend to express our individual dark-skinned selves without fear or shame." His poetry embraced and in fact exulted in the gift of his African ancestry. His poetry reflected the music and rhythms of his people, making the powerful point that "no great poet has ever been afraid of being himself."

Not surprisingly he was one of the "shakers and movers" of what was called "the Harlem Renaissance," after the section of New York City inhabited by so many black artists and musicians. Between the world wars this area was almost a black kingdom unto itself, but everyone, white or black, appreciated the vitality of life, the pulsing energy that flowed outwards from Harlem. It was exciting, and it spread its influence throughout American culture, particularly the energy of its music and dance. Langston Hughes was right in the middle of it.

He was turning his back on his bondage. He was free. He fought for his country in World War II. He was a great poet for his time. He was an All-American.

Mother to Son

(Langston Hughes, 1902-1967)

Well, son, I'll tell you:
Life for me ain't been no crystal stair.
It's had tacks in it,
And splinters,
And boards torn up,
And places with no carpet on the floor—
Bare.
But all the time
I'se been climbin' on,
And reachin' landin's,
And turnin' corners,
And sometimes goin' in the dark
Where they ain't been no light.
So boy, don't you turn back.
Don't you set down on the steps
'Cause you finds it's kinder hard.
Don't you fall now—
For I'se still goin', honey,
I'se still climbin',
And life for me ain't been no crystal stair.

HAS THIS MOTHER'S LIFE BEEN
A.) EASY
B.) HARD OR
C.) VERY HARD

DID SHE GIVE UP?

WHAT SORT OF AN EXAMPLE HAS THIS MOM BEEN FOR HER SON?

DOES THIS POEM MAKE YOU THINK THAT
1.) LIFE IS NOTHING BUT FUN
2.) YOU CAN SIMPLY 'TAKE IT EASY.'
3.) YOU MUST HAVE FAITH IN YOURSELF
4.) YOU SHOULD NOT GIVE UP WHEN IT SEEMS "HARD."
(PICK TWO OF THE ABOVE)

IF YOU WERE STRUGGLING TO ACHIEVE SOME GOAL, AND WERE DISCOURAGED, AND THOUGHT OF GIVING UP, WHAT WOULD READING THIS POEM SAY TO YOU?

Terms on p. 94

DYLAN THOMAS (1914-1953)

I am down to the wire. This "course" must end. I must stop before you become seventh graders. But whom can I not leave out? Who do I have to believe, that for pure poetic passion and a mastery of the most colorful words in their richest combinations, is the greatest poetic genius of the mid-twentieth century? Who is like a comet streaking "his blazing tail" across the dark sky where other poets seem but bright stars? And who comes from a Celtic tradition famous for its eloquence, poetry, and song? Who wrote that charming book-poem that you may have received once for Christmas, entitled "A Child's Christmas in Wales"?

YOUNG AND EASY

Obviously, the answer is Dylan Thomas, one of the most incandescent of poetry's many flamboyant personalities. And yes, like a comet he burned himself out, mostly by spending too much not very sober time in various bar-rooms, particularly in the final decade of his life when he was living in New York. The only way he could quench the flame that seemed to burn so intensely within him was, apparently, with alcohol. He was dead by the age of 39, his liver destroyed by heavy drinking.

It was possibly poetry that kept him going for as long as he did. It was one of his true passions, the other two being drinking and talking. And what a wonderful talker he was, or at least so I have heard. And what a rich, resonant voice he possessed, like so many of the Welsh. His readings of his own poetry are famous, and his recordings thrill the listening ear. No, sadly, I never heard him talk myself, but when I was in college, near New York, we would all find a way into the city, and sneak down to the bars where we thought Dylan Thomas hung out, hoping we would catch a sight or sound of him. I never did. I had a friend, however, who claimed to have been extravagantly insulted by Dylan Thomas, on one of his drunken binges in some downtown bar.

That, of course, is worth nothing. You must not believe everything people tell you. Even so, my friend was envied and admired, for any of us would have given a tooth to have been insulted by the living Dylan Thomas, drunk or sober.

As for choosing a poem that would be a good example of Thomas's work, I do not have to worry. Any of them will do. Immediately you will be struck by the impact of his words, of their emotional content and power, of their luxuriant quality. His poem, "A Refusal to Mourn the Death, by Fire, of a Child in London" is one of the most poignant to have come out of World War Two. The first line of the poem that begins "Do not go gentle into that good night" has become a part of our common landscape of words. But "Fern Hill" is the one for us, because it is about childhood and growing up. Nor need you, by the way, be alarmed by the suggestion in the last stanza that time, and growing up, inevitably steals from you what is "green and carefree" in childhood. It may steal from some, but it need steal from you, if you can remember to keep yourself "young at heart."

But not, as maybe Dylan Thomas did, by dosing yourself with whiskey. Whiskey rots your liver. When Ogden Nash famously wrote "Candy is dandy, but liquor is quicker," what do you think he meant by "quicker"? Quicker to where?

64

Fern Hill

(Dylan Thomas, 1914-1953)

Now as I was young and easy under the apple bows,
About the lilting house and happy as the grass was green,
   The night above the dingle starry,
     Time let me hail and climb
    Golden in the heydays of his eyes,
And honored among the wagons I was prince of the apple towns
And once below a time I lordly had the trees and leaves
     Trail with daisies and barley
    Down the rivers of the windfall light.

And as I was green and carefree, famous among the barns
About the happy yard and singing as the farm was home,
  In the sun that is young once only.
    Time let me play and be
  Golden in the mercy of his means,
And green and golden I was huntsman and herdsman, the calves
Sang to my horn, the foxes on the hills barked clear and cold,
    And the Sabbath rang slowly
  In the pebbles of the holy streams.

All the sun long it was running, it was lovely, the hay
Fields high as the house, the tunes from the chimneys, it was air
  And playing, lovely and watery
    And fire green as grass.
  And nightly under the simple stars
As I rode to sleep the owls wee bearing the farm away,
All the moon long I heard, blessed among stables, the nightjars
  Flying with the ricks, and the horses
    Flashing into the dark.

And then to awake, and the farm, like a wanderer white
With the dew, come back, the cock on his shoulder: it was all
  Shining, it was Adam and maiden,
    The sky gathered again
  And the sun grew round that very day.
So it must have been after the birth of the simple light
In the first, spinning place, the spellbound horses walking warm
  Out of the whinnying green stable
    On to the fields of praise.

And honored among foxes and pheasants by the gay house
Under the new made clouds and happy as the heart was long,
  In the sun born over and over,
    I ran my heedless ways,
  My wishes raced through the house high hay
And nothing I cared, at my sky blue trades, that time allows
In all his tuneful turning so few and such morning songs
  Before the children green and golden
    Follow him out of grace.

Nothing I cared, in the lamb white days, that time would take me
Up to the swallow thronged loft by the shadow of my hand,
  In the moon that is always rising,
    Nor that riding to sleep
  I should hear him fly with the high fields
And wake to the farm forever fled from the childless land.
Oh as I was young and easy in the mercy of his means,
   Time held me green and dying
    Though I sang in my chains like the sea.

TELL ME, IN HIS CHILDHOOD DOES IT SOUND LIKE THOMAS IS

A.) HAVING FUN
B.) CAREFREE
C.) RUNNING ABOUT
D.) CLIMBING APPLE TREES
E.) EXCITED WITH LIFE
F.) FILLED WITH WONDER
G.) LIVING IN A GREEN & GOLDEN MOMENT
H.) THOUGHTLESS
I.) UNWORRIED
J.) FULL OF ENERGY
K.) HONORED AMONG FOXES
L.) ALL OF THE ABOVE

BUT WHAT DOES THOMAS THINK TIME KILLS?

65

DR. SEUSS (1904-1991)

Whatever 'tis

That poetry IS,

I'm more than sure

Dr. Seuss's is.

But that, in the first place, is a "so what?" In the second place, you can tell me, maybe better than I know, whether or not Dr. Seuss wrote "poetry." I am going to say he did, and insist on his being included in this "course."

Poetry, like grand opera, unfortunately sometimes gets itself surrounded by the idea that it is pretty high-fallutin' stuff. It might be OK for odd ducks and the occasional nerd who for some strange reason may prefer it to football, but on the whole many actual people find it just a bit incomprehensible. It does not seem immediately "easy." It is not as conveniently grasped and swallowed as, for example, a bag of potato chips. We have been privileged, perhaps, to live in a world that has been happy to cater to our convenience. We are insulated, air-conditioned, auto-mobilized, and televisionized. Surrounded by the magic of Nature, the glory of God, and the possibility of Love, all of which throughout the ages poets have written of, we tend to turn on the TV and reach for another Dorito.

IN A HAT . . .

We have been "privileged" with excess, which obscures and causes us to forget the bright miracle of our lives, and all that lives and is. As Gerard Manley Hopkins, a wonderful English poet who was a contemporary of Emily Dickinson, and like her also "before his time," wrote

The world is charged with the grandeur of God

It will flame out, like shining from shook foil."

Hopkins, Dickinson, all poets, honor this miracle in the words they select to try to do it justice.

And so did Dr. Seuss. It has been rightly said that he should get a Nobel Prize for literature. It has been judged by some that his stories are not poems, but somehow they seem to be. Is it his drawings of those odd scruffy animals and humans who all look the same, or his words, that make his point? It is almost as though he is a "Poet" who, because he was writing for small children, extended their limited vocabulary into drawing. The "poetry" lies in each and both together, a happy balance of the right lines, and the right words, in the right places.

That, when it captures the world and reflects it back so well, is surely a goodly part of what poetry is. It does not matter if the world you know is six or sixty years of age.

Just call it poetry. Or at least call it "green eggs and ham, Sam."

"The Grinch Who Stole Christmas"
("Dr. Seuss", born Theodor Seusss Geisel, 1904-1991)

The Grinch *hated* Christmas! The whole Christmas season!
Now, please don't ask why. No one quite knows the reason.
It *could* be his head wasn't screwed on just right.
It *could* be, perhaps, that his shoes were too tight.
But I think that the most likely reason of all
May have been that his heart was two sizes too small.
But,
Whatever the reason,
His heart or his shoes,
He stood there on Christmas Eve, hating the *Whos*,
Staring down from his cave with a sour, Grinchy frown
At the warm lighted windows below in their town.
For he knew every *Who* down in *Who*-ville beneath
Was busy now, hanging a mistletoe wreath…..

…..

Then the Grinch thought of something he hadn't before!
"Maybe Christmas," he thought, "doesn't come from a store.
Maybe Christmas…perhaps…means a little bit more!"
And what happened then…?
Well, in Who-ville they say
That the Grinch's small heart
Grew three sizes that day!
And the minute his heart didn't feel quite so tight,
He whizzed with his load through the bright morning light,
And he brought back the toys! And the food for the feast!
    And he…
    …HE HIMSELF…!
The Grinch carves the roast beast!

NO NEED TO ADD
A WORD TO THIS /

CHARLES EDWARDS MOORE (1934- :O))

I have always dreamed of winning the lottery, but since I have never bought a ticket, I think my chances of winning are slimmer than for those who do. I have also always dreamed, and far more than about "winning the lottery," of writing a poem, such as "I Think Continually of Those Who Are Truly Great," that some anthologist would think brilliant enough to include in a collection of poetry.

But if you don't write a poem it is for sure not going into any anthology. You have to do it. And so I have, just a little. In my life I have written maybe thirty poems, half of which were half-finished and lost, and half of the other half simply lost. That leaves maybe seven, if I can find them.

5:30 A.M.

Well, you may think it a little "sneaky," but I am about to fulfill my own poetic ambition. Because I have appointed myself my own anthologist, having chosen the very poems in this collection we have studied, I permit myself to include one of my very own poems in it. So there! You clearly see that to do something takes simply doing it! "Here error," as we recall the words of Pound, "is all in the not doing, all in the diffidence that faltered." Dauntlessly, I now find myself in a veritable anthology just where I have always wanted to be. Thus and so it comes about that "a Blunt should open."

Come to think of it, this little poem about a milkman derives a little from Pound himself, and the sometimes exotic and rather sensual images he used, particularly in some of his early poems describing luxurious ladies, like even Cleopatra. Such imagery seems very far removed from the "milkman," but that, of course, is part of the fun of poetry: that out of the grandeur of your own experience you can relate, and thereby endow with almost new meaning, ordinarily "commonplace" events and things.

Let me share with you a little background. None of you, and not even I, except dimly, remember a time when the milkman came to your door at the crack of dawn and left you fresh milk in real glass bottles. Your Mom or Dad would put the empty bottles out on the doorstep, with a little note saying how many bottles of fresh milk or cream you needed for that day. In those now bygone days there was not the refrigeration, nor the big supermarkets we have grown so used to today. Originally, the milk was delivered in horse-drawn wagons full of ice, and later (for habits do die hard) in little milk trucks that substituted mechanical refrigeration for ice. But customs do die, replaced perhaps by something better, but leaving in their wake a wistful memory.

England, where my sister lives, is famous for maintaining these memories and traditions, not only in having a Queen, but even down to retaining the milkman. Accordingly, while I was visiting my sister who lives in England, the milkman attracted my attention. It was just dawn, still dark, and I was half asleep in the little downstairs bedroom by the front steps. I heard the truck. I heard the crunch of the feet on the gravel. I heard the pause as the milkman read the note. Another pause, then the rattle of the bottles. The milkman had come, it seemed to me, out of the misty past.

WHOSE REAL NAME WAS THEOPHRASTUS PHILLIPPUS AUREOLUS BOMBASTUS VON HOHENHEIM LIVING FROM 1493 to 1541.

5.30 AM. It is...

(Charles E. Moore, 1934-the living present)

HE WAS NOT ONLY A FAMOUS, AND NOTORIOUS, PHYSICIAN IN HIS TIME, HOLDING AND WRITING AT GREAT LENGTH ON MANY CONTROVERSIAL IDEAS HE HAD ABOUT MEDICINE, BUT SOUGHT THE SECRETS OF LIFE THROUGH MAGIC & ALCHEMY

It is the milkman,
Merely bringing the green grass
Of England's greenest fields,
Transmuted by the alchemy of the cow
Into more than gold.
Paracelsus, failing, yet sought no more,
For who is the infant wizard
To refuse his Mother's milk?

OUR WORD 'BOMBAST', MEANING TO TALK WITH A HIGH-SOUNDING, INFLATED, BRAGGING STYLE COMES FROM 'PARACELSUS' NAME.

Even the Gods,
In the white radiance of their eternity,
On this and honey fed.
And did not Cleopatra,
Almond-eyed upon her gorgeous barge
Bathe in it her alabaster skin,
Thereby preparing the conquest of her conqueror.

And now, aroused from sleep
By the sound of the milkman's steps
Upon the gravel-stones, I wake
To bless his image,
Pay homage to his cows,
And the pastures of this green and sceptered isle,
Bottled, and in the dream
Of this midsummer night
Delivered here, to the very doorstep
Of my sweet desire.

THAT WAS HOW HE WROTE

AND THOUGH HE SOUNDED GRAND, AND WROTE A GREAT DEAL, HE NEVER TURNED LEAD INTO GOLD... NOR EVEN GRASS INTO MILK, AS A COW CAN !

69

EPILOGUE

So there we have it. But what, you may ask, is IT?

Well, first off, IT has been a little poetry course exposing you to some BIG names, except for the last, which is no name at all, in the course of our English language poetic tradition. There is nothing wrong and a great deal right with this bit of knowledge.

Secondly, it is just possible that you may have learned something about the meaning of poetry, both in the life of the poet and in that of the reader. Poetry is a way of sharing a vision of this miracle of a universe we live in, and are such a part of. It uses words arranged on a page as carefully as a painter puts paint to a canvas, to create not only a memorable image of the world, but one that enhances your own and others' appreciation of it.

But how does one go about writing a poem? We have only barely touched on the act of writing an occasional poem or bit of verse yourself.

Everyone, of course, is different. Every painter is differently prompted to paint, and each has a different way of painting. So, too, with poetic composition. I can only speak, and at that just a little, for myself. The first things that you need, for sure, are a writing instrument, a bit of paper, and some quiet time. For myself, just as with the poem "5.30 AM," which actually is about that very moment as well as the magic of how green grass gets changed into white milk, I tend to get a little idea in an early, half-woken moment of the morning. Sleep has washed away all the debris from the day before that had preoccupied me. I vaguely wake up, and maybe begin to think about some little fragment of experience that floats upwards onto the brain's surface. Suddenly there may come a little line, and maybe another that follows it. If I like it, and don't want to fall back to sleep and thereby forget these struggling words, I get up and write them down. Often, and maybe quickly, as with "5.30 AM," more may follow. But sometimes a "first line" may pop up right in the middle of the day, too. Jot it down.

And so you get a start. Without the start, there is no ending. Many times, in fact, you may not bring your poem to completion. But that's all right. Sometimes a poem may take a long time, even years, in the creation. Many may remain only parts of poems. But even so, within those fragments, themselves worth saving in some shoebox, is some sort of poetic record of yourself, your perception and involvement with the world. With a little practice, and a little thought, hardly more than it takes to play some game, your skills at both seeing the world, and exploring yourself, will improve. And so you become a poet. More and more, you enjoy the sounds and meanings of words, just as a trained musician can appreciate the subtle pleasure of musical notes in their right places.[1] And you do not need a piano or a big bassoon, or even a tube of paint. A bit of pencil and a scrap of paper will quite do.

So, let me suggest, write it down. One day you may have a lovely poem in an anthology, without, as I have had to do, creating the anthology itself to achieve that triumph.

---

[1] I am not thinking here of "Rock" or "Bee-Bop" or "Heavy Metal," but, I beg you, something more classical, like Mozart.

70

GLOSSARY

Following is a bunch of words or names, noted also in the right hand margin of your "text," whose meanings I have put here totally for your complete and happy convenience. You may already know most of them, some of them, all of them, or almost none of them. It doesn't matter. They are simply here, take 'em or leave 'em. If you are really brave, and "take 'em," that is to say actually look here to find words you do not know, you have my congratulations. If you don't know a word, and I have left it out, you must forgive me if I say to you, "Too bad! You'll have to look it up in a real dictionary."

As for a "Glossary," who can tell me what it is? I am NOT including it in these definitions. You will have to look it up. (Ha-Ha!) On the other hand, maybe you can figure it out for yourself from this example. Even if you do not read a single poem, or learn about a single poet, you will know for sure what a "glossary" is. And who knows? Maybe the Glossary itself will tempt you to read a poem after all. . . .

PREFACE

Admonitions: Warnings. "To admonish" is to warn, or even to scold, as when some enormous adult, like a parent for example, stands before you shaking a huge finger at you, telling you to do this or that . . . or ELSE!" The "or else" is anything the parent can think of that sounds threatening, like room restriction for the rest of your life.

CHAUCER

Gaelic (GAY-lick): A rather complicated language, for those unfamiliar with it, to speak or spell. It is full of double letters where you least expect them. Gaelic is still used in parts of Scotland, Ireland, and Wales by the descendents of the people called the Celts, who populated the British Isles before the invasion by the Romans 2000 years ago. Although the English language came mostly from Latin, German, and French, there are a few words that drifted into it from the Gaelic, such as *neamhbhásmhaireacht*, but not very many, mostly because no one can pronounce them.

Diplomat: A fine figure of a gentleman or lady, who represents a country when talks are being held with other countries. The art of **diplomacy** has to do with saying just the right thing, in order to get what you want without letting the other **diplomat** take from you what you don't want to give. Good **diplomacy**, however, usually ends up in some sort of compromise. A good **diplomat** has to be rather clever, and good with words. He or she should not look like a slob either. You are, by the way, constantly in **diplomatic** contact with your teachers. Parents, also, frequently require an artful application of **diplomatic** skills.

Ambassador: An **ambassador**, as you may already know, or at least I would guess you might know, is a very great diplomat, who has been selected to be the chief representative from one country to another, and who has perhaps a very large staff appointed to assist him. Examples are our **ambassadors** to France, Russia, and China. The ambassadorship is a very important post, requiring a shrewd mind and eye. It also requires an ability to go to lots of social functions that you don't really want to go to at all, in order to make a good impression for your country. Ambassadors work pretty hard, and the strain of always looking and sounding just perfect probably demands that they take lots of naps.

Canterbury: A lovely little city in the southeastern corner of England, long known and made famous by the Canterbury Cathedral, which was built immediately following the Norman Conquest of England in 1066 and much expanded in the centuries following. Canterbury and its lovely cathedral are, like Rome and the Vatican for the Catholic Church, the "seat" of the Anglican Church, from which the Episcopal Church in the United States sprang. In Chaucer's time, even before Henry the Eighth founded the Anglican Church, people flocked to Canterbury on pilgrimages to say their prayers and to have a nice little vacation at the same time. People still are eager to go there when they visit England, because of the long religious history that is part of the place, and also because of the beauty of the ancient cathedral.

SHAKESPEARE

Conjunction: Any word that joins other words together. The words "and," "but" and "or" are called **conjunctions**, as you well know from your study of grammar. They bridge between or join together two phrases within a sentence, connecting them, or conjoining them.

Surpassingly: Everyone who knows what the verb **to surpass** means, please raise your hand. Quite so. Everyone knows. I should have left this one out. **To surpass**, of course, means to go beyond. If your teacher says that "your work is **surpassingly** good," immediately ask her to put her comment in writing, frame it, and show your parents, because it means you have done wonderfully well, 'way beyond anyone else.

Innumerable: Countless, of course. Almost beyond numbering. This is easy.

Queen Elizabeth the First: This is easy, too. Everyone knows who she is, the strong lady with a ruff around her neck (what is a ruff?), who was Queen during one of England's most glorious ages. Did you see the movie "**Elizabeth**"? She lived from 1533 to 1603. When did Shakespeare die?

Sir Walter Raleigh: A great courtier in Elizabeth's court, and also a great writer, poet, historian, and explorer-adventurer. He was supposed to have "spread his cloak," and a very pricey one it was, too, over a mud puddle for Elizabeth the Queen to step upon so as not to muddy her shoes and skirts. That is a fine story, but who knows what really happened? On the other hand what really did happen was that he lost his head. Under suspicion of treason, he was given one final commission to prove his loyalty and worth to the crown. He was to command an expedition to search for, discover, and bring back several shiploads of gold from the fabled land of El Dorado in South America. He sallied forth with a tiny fleet, hoping for new glory, but he found only defeat. The venture was a disaster. He found neither El Dorado nor gold, came back disgraced, and was once again imprisoned in the Tower. He languished for years in prison, during which time he wrote some of his finest poetry and a "History of the World." Finally, he had his head rather rudely chopped off by James the First, who had become king after Elizabeth had died. "I am but dust," he wrote in his last letter to his wife, and in his poem, "A Farewell to the Vanities of the World," he summarized his life's disappointments, writing

> FAREWELL, ye gilded follies, pleasing troubles!
> Farewell, ye honored rags, ye glorious bubbles!
> Fame's but a hollow echo; gold, pure clay;
> Honor, the darling but of one short day.

As was the tradition of the time, his wife was given his head, which she had pickled and carried with her everywhere she went until her own death at age 82.

Sir Francis Drake: Perhaps the greatest and most swashbuckling of the great Elizabethan sea-captains. He bested the Spanish, who were more-or-less at war constantly with England, in many sea battles, stole their gold, became a great hero, and was the first Englishman ever to sail around the world in his little ship, "The Golden Hind." (A hind is a female red deer, fleet of foot.) He was the first to discover San Francisco Bay, and is thought to have left a plaque buried there somewhere. To search for it would be a fine project for you, and if you could discover it you would become archeologically famous.

DONNE

St. Paul's Cathedral: A famous church in London. One or another church of this name has been on the present site in London ever since 604 A.D. The cathedral Chaucer would have known was finished in 1310. Burned down in the Great Fire of London in 1666, it was rebuilt to according to the design of the very famous architect Sir Christopher Wren, and its dome rivaled that of St. Peter's Cathedral in Rome. During World War Two, when Nazi bombers destroyed so much of the part of London immediately surrounding St. Paul's, the dome still stood, and photographs of it rising above the smoke and flames became an inspiring image of Britain's will never to surrender to the Nazis.

Contemporaries: Yes, of course. When something is **contemporary** it means it is at the same time as something else, most frequently you and me. You and I are **contemporaries** because we live at the same time in history. John Donne was a **contemporary** of James the First of England, who was king when Donne was writing his poetry. Sometimes the term **contemporary** stands for 'modern,' too, that is, 'belonging to the present time,' just as you do, and maybe I do, too.

Portrait: You all know, I am sure, that a **portrait** is nothing more than a picture of a person. But often the term is used to describe a more formal sort of picture, where one is dressed in one's best, and the photographer or artist who creates the picture charges a lot more money than you would ever get for a simple snapshot of yourself and your pet turtle.

MILTON

Contrived: The past tense of the verb **to contrive,** which means to plan, design, create, make. When you make up a funny April Fool's trick, like for example substituting salt for the sugar in the sugar bowl, or when you dream up a really scary Halloween costume, you are **contriving**, and whatever you dream up or make is your **contrivance**.

Epic: A great story, usually on a grand, majestic, legendary scale. Homer's *Iliad* and *Odyssey* were the first great epics of western poetry. In our time the "Star Wars" series of films made by George Lucas are part of the **epic** tradition of story telling, full of great deeds by great heroes fighting against terrible odds.

Venerated: The past tense of the verb **to venerate**, meaning to honor, worship, even adore. What you **venerate**, of course, needs to deserve **veneration**. For example, you do not particularly **venerate** a worm; but on the other hand, one does **venerate** 'Life,' and therefore all things living, so even a worm's life may deserve honest respect, and particularly if he (or she, who can tell?) is a pleasant, well-behaved worm.

DRYDEN

Aspire: To desire, to want, to seek, to work toward. Usually this word implies that you are working towards a positive or lofty goal, like being in the Olympics, or earning the best grades in your class, or acquiring a lofty reputation for excellence of character or behavior. No one you or I know would ever **aspire**, on the other hand, to becoming a crazed drug addict who has burnt out his brain.

Dabble: To fool around, to do anything in a slight, superficial manner, like splashing in the water with your hands. You should never **dabble**, of course, with your studies, but take them very seriously except for, perhaps, this course, which is designed specifically for **dabbling** in a bit of poetry.

Abide: To adhere to, to strictly obey or follow. In the Bible, who said "**abide** by me"?

Etiquette: Rules of social behavior. Every age and culture has its own special codes of behavior, and some cultures might severely punish you for breaking them. In our own time we are quite liberal and permissive in allowing people to look and act just any old way they want. Even so, and even now, who wants to be a slob without any manners, or consideration of others? In Dryden's time, how you behaved in society was a very important part of who you were. Conformity to strict standards of dress and decorum, particularly at Court, was necessary, or else you would be tossed out, as they say, on your ear.

Decorum: The way in which a person with the finest manners behaves. In Dryden's time the taking of a lady's hand, or the gracefulness of a bow with your knee bent and leg extended just so, was good etiquette, and such fine displays of **decorum** were much admired. Nowadays we think of all those fancy forms as being stuffy and even a little silly. But to Dryden and his contemporaries there was nothing silly about them at all. On the other hand Dryden, if he could observe our modern behavior, would probably think it equally silly that we should wear a baseball cap with the bill facing backwards. Or what about sideways? Do you prefer to the left or right? Why?

Maestro: The name given to a master of any art, most particularly to a great composer or conductor of an orchestra. People often compare the universe, as Dryden did, to a great symphony, in which all the notes or atoms fit together in 'celestial harmony.' In that view, God is the **Maestro** over all, conducting, as it was called, "The Music of the Spheres." (What "spheres"? Name one. Do you live on one?)

POPE

Poet Laureate: A **laureate** is someone who is crowned, honored, "the winner." The word derives from the laurel tree, which grows in southern Europe. In ancient Greece, leaves from this tree were made into crowns and placed on the heads of the winners of the Olympic Games. In 1619, when Donne was at the height of his powers, a coin was minted in England depicting King James I with such a crown on his head, and this coin was accordingly called a "laurel." A country's **Poet Laureate** is a poet chosen above all to be honored for his or her work. When you graduate from college you will get a "Bacca**laureate**," which means you have "won the laurel" and gained your Bachelor of Arts or Science degree.

In the old days, a "crown of **laurel**" was a great honor and recompense for winning athletes, but now they just get money.

The Iliad and *The Odyssey*: Of course you know about the Trojan War, and how Odysseus had so many wild adventures and narrow escapes in all those long years it took him to get back to Ithaca, and his wife Penelope, after it was over. If you do not, I will have to send you back to the fifth grade. These great poetic epics were created at the very beginnings of the literary tradition of western civilization. Along with the Bible, Shakespeare, and Dante's *The Divine Comedy*, Homer, who lived before all of them, 3000 years ago, has had the most profound influence on who we now are, how we write, what we write, and how we think about our world.

Grotto: A sort of cave, rather dark and mysterious, often in some wild and forsaken place. **Grottos** were sometimes inhabited by hermits, and at one time it became fashionable to have one on your grounds. If you were a great "Lord" with sufficient "grounds," a **grotto**, and even a "hermit" you might "rent" to inhabit it, was very fashionable. A **grotto**, and I suppose particularly one with a real fake hermit, was supposed to remind people that living simply and naturally had something "divine" about it, to be admired if not aspired to for yourself. After all, every time you looked out your window and spied the hermit living in his cold, dark **grotto**, it reminded you of how lucky you yourself were not to have to live in such an uncomfortable hole in the ground. Pope was very proud of his **grotto**, even though it did not have a hermit, and he relished showing it off to his guests.

Heroic couplet: A couplet is a term applied to verse when two consecutive lines, each with the same number of 'beats," rhyme. Why some couplets are called "heroic," I am not sure. It may be because they were popular when poets were writing mostly about great heroes like Odysseus.

GRAY

Elegy: This word comes to us from the ancient Greek word *elegos*, a lament. It is the term given to any poem of sorrow, or praise for the dead, or as in this case any poem written in a mournful, thoughtful manner.

Meditation: I should probably not waste the poor Glossary's space including this word. Everyone knows what **meditate** means, for it has become a popular "sport" among people inclined to find a means of calming themselves down. Of course, **meditation** is a nice thing to do in a haphazard, busy world. A little **meditation**, so to speak, allows the mind, body, and spirit a little rest. Beyond that, a **meditation** is also a solemn reflection on any subject, often religious, but not necessarily. I have always considered the film "Cannibal Women in the Avocado Jungle of Death" one of the best **meditations** on the subject of the relationship between the sexes, a very serious, if not altogether solemn, subject.

Eloquent: Beautifully put, gracefully spoken, forcefully stated, either in speech or writing. In older days **eloquence** of language was very much prized, and carefully studied as well as practiced. Nowadays, we mostly just have "sound bites" on television, which are more or less the opposite of **eloquence**. Even so, **eloquence** is by no means a "lost art." You can practice a little **eloquence** now and again on, for example, your parents and teachers, and perhaps thus astonish them. The last truly great practitioner of **eloquence** in the making and giving of speeches was Sir Winston Churchill. He adored the English language, and used it to very powerful effect in the words he addressed to the English people during the dark days of 1940, when England stood alone against the Nazis.

Acclaim: To applaud, salute, cry out in favor of. A cheer is a loud and great **acclamation**. To whom do you give the most **acclaim** in your life? You might attempt, of course, to give your parents a little, but there is nothing wrong with giving great **acclaim** to your middle school teachers either, without, of course, being a "brown nose"...which I will not discuss at all.

Beguiled (be-GUYld): To be **beguiled** is to be misled, but usually by a rather charming means, which combines both amusement and temptation. Pinocchio was much **beguiled** by that bad fox, who entertained him with all sorts of agreeable notions about what a wonderful place "Fun Island" would be, but it wasn't, was it? I was once, myself, actually **beguiled** by a young lady, who led me along with my own idiocy into much distress, by which I mean to suggest that one must also be careful, most particularly, perhaps, when one finds oneself taking the next step beyond **beguilement**, and becomes an idiot. We can, after all, cast a spell even upon our very own selves, and be led down what is called a "Primrose Path" to "Fun Island," which does not turn out to be fun at all. (Remember Pinocchio? What animal tempted him to go to "Fun Island"? A rabbit? A snake? A fox? A Labrador retriever?)

Pembroke College, Cambridge: The Universities of Oxford and Cambridge, dating back to the 12th and 13th centuries, were organized around subunits called "Colleges," which governed themselves independently. Each College came to attract its own sort of student, and thereby developed its own flavor and personality. Cambridge was famous for producing many of England's greatest poets, and many of these, including Thomas Gray, came from **Pembroke College**.

Melancholic (mel-an-KOLL-ick): *Melas* and *Melanos* are forms of the Greek word meaning "black," and the *chole* part also comes from the Greek, meaning "bile." Accordingly, in its origin, **melancholy** means "black bile." Just two or three centuries ago, physicians thought that health was based on the balance between the four "humours" (liquids) that existed in the body, "black bile," "yellow bile," "blood" and "phlegm." Your personality was even thought to be dictated by whether or not you had too much of one or the other of these elements. A person with too much "black bile" was of a depressed, sad, gloomy, and irritable temper. Gray was none of this, but his poem is **melancholic** because it is sort of sad, meditative, and set in a graveyard. We are all of us affected from time to time with an occasional melancholic feeling, aren't we?

Ode: A poem, usually rather long, addressed in a complimentary fashion to some person or thing. It is often written in a lofty style, rich with the dignity and eloquence of its words. On the other hand, an **ode** might be quite brief, and even simple, if its words beautifully hit just the right and honest mark. Gray, who wrote an "**Ode**" on the death of his cat, was using the term rather playfully, "tongue-in-cheek,," for a dead cat, even one much loved, is NOT the usual subject for a "lofty style." On the other hand, Shelley (who comes along later) wrote an "Ode to the West Wind," which is a famous example of the form. Let us hope that the "West Wind" was appreciative, and maybe even brought some rain in a dry season.

Elegaic (el-uh-JYE-ick): Well, you already know all about this. **Elegaic** is the adjective form of "Elegy," and so an "**elegaic** cow" would either be simply a sad cow, or otherwise a cow standing not in its proper field, but in the middle of an "Elegy." This is, of course, exactly what Gray's cows are so famous for doing, as well as (when Gray was not looking) mooing, or as he described it "lowing," which is a kind of quiet mooing.

Derive: To discover the origin of something, to work out how something came from something else to be what it finally is, to take from what was and make from what you next make it. Darwin, for example, said that "Man" was **derived** from the monkey. The Bible says we **derive** from God. Science might say we **derive** from atoms that came from the stars. A plant **derives** from its seed. My cotton shirt **derives** from a plant. The whole process of life is one of **derivation**.

BLAKE

Archangels: Angels of the highest rank, ruling over all the other Angels just as Archbishops rule over all other Bishops. For your interest, even though you will NOT be tested on this subject, this is the Angelic hierarchy, from Topmost-Angel to Littlest-Angel: Cherubims, Seraphims, and Thrones along with Lords, Powers, and Rulers involve themselves with the very highest affairs of the Divine Spirit. Principalities, Archangels, and Angels take care of "created things," from insects on up to elephants and ourselves. In any case, as Richard Wilbur, a famous contemporary American poet, wrote in a lovely poem:

>...Outside the open window
>The morning air is all awash with angels.
>   Some are in bed-sheets, some are in blouses
>Some are in smocks: but truly there they are.
>Now they are rising together in calm swells
>Of halcyon feeling, filling whatever they wear
>With the deep joy of their impersonal breathing;
>   Now they are flying in place, conveying
>The terrible speed of their omnipresence, moving
>And staying like white water; and now of a sudden
>They swoon down into so rapt a quiet
>That nobody seems to be there....

Virgil: If you wanted to add another great name to those of Homer, Dante, and Shakespeare, you might well think of **Virgil**. He was to the classical Romans and the Latin language what Shakespeare is to us and English. Virgil's *Aeneid*, written in the century before Christ was born, is an epic poem about the foundation of Rome after the Trojan War. It almost defines for us the use of the term "Epic" as applied to poetry. And even though **Virgil** wrote his Epic in Latin (naturally!) his style was of such distinctive clarity that English writers, particularly in the 18th century, looked to **Virgil** as their finest example. The result was that the English of that century was and remains to this day famous for its eloquence. For three hundred years and more, English schoolchildren at the 6th grade level studied Latin so that they could, by reading **Virgil**, learn all the better to write English! (By the way, some folks spell his name **Vergil**.)

Horace: Another famous Roman author. He was a contemporary of Virgil, and was also much admired for his writing style. Aside from his poetry, **Horace** is fascinating to us because his country villa, situated in a lovely valley near Licenza some miles east of Rome, has come down to us for study and archeological excavation. It was discovered and identified as his in the 18th century thanks to the precise (and lovely) descriptions of it that **Horace** wrote. **Horace** was proud of his country house and loved entertaining there. For the interest of those of you who enjoy reading a little Latin, **Horace** wrote a story called *Two Roman Mice*, about a town-mouse and a country-mouse, beautifully illustrated and retold by Marilynne K. Roach in an edition published in 1977. Get onto the Web, and you will find it under "**Horace**."

George Washington: Really, now! Never mind! But wait: Think about him a moment! Of all the people who founded our nation, from his soldiers and friends to all of the citizens of our new country, **Washington** most perfectly embodied the bearing, dignity, and selfless patriotism that was applauded and acclaimed by the ancient Romans. If the writings of Thomas Jefferson were deeply influenced by the style of Latin authors such as Horace and Vergil, so were the bearing and manner of George Washington modeled on the ideals of "the Noble Roman." Indeed, Washington actually had his portrait painted draped in a Roman toga. Thus, you see, how much we still derive from ages past!

Hallucinations: From the Latin (once again!), *hallucinatio,* meaning "to rave, to wander in the mind." A hallucination is a perception of sights or sounds that are not actually there. Drugs and alcohol can cause horrible **hallucinations**. It might sound sort of funny to see "pink elephants," but no one really wants to see them, or smell their breath when they are trumpeting in your face. Such a **hallucination** would then be visual (you see it), auditory (you hear it), and olefactory (you smell it).

Bedlam: A famous lunatic asylum, or mental hospital, originally founded in 1247 by the religious order of "The Star of Bethlehem." In 1547, when all the monasteries in England were dissolved by King Henry the Eighth, the Bethlehem asylum was given to the City of London as a hospital for the insane. The name became in due course shortened to **Bedlam**. The poor people imprisoned there were, by our standards, most cruelly treated, and adding insult to injury it became a sort of fashionable social "outing" to visit Bedlam, to look at, and even mock the inmates, who in their pitiful state would roar and howl like animals. Accordingly, in modern use, "**bedlam**" defines a scene where uproar and confusion are taking place.

BURNS

Doughty (DOW-tee): Brave. Eminent. Famous. A doughty person is one who is capable of performing wonderful deeds. Achilles and Charles Lindbergh were **doughty** heroes, and one might say the same for Luke Skywalker. But today the use of this term, which is somewhat old-fashioned and out of style, contains the suggestion that the "hero" is also somehow rather entertaining or even amusing. In some of his films Eddie Murphy is *quite* "the **doughty** hero."

Wrought: This is the alternative past tense of the verb "to work," or "to form, fashion, make." **Wrought** itself is a little archaic, which means "old-fashioned and out-of-date," but it is fun to use, and that is why I use it. Words can only be kept alive, remember, by their use, and though many words have died, they (as another poet, Dylan Thomas wrote) need not "go gentle into that good night." In this use relating to the Norsemen, they did for sure in their day work a very great deal of devastation across the lands they invaded. **Wrought** remains very much with us in the use of the term "wrought-iron."

Havoc: An activity that leads to destruction and ruin. In olden times when armies besieged a city and forced their way through the city's walls, the signal **cry havoc** would be given, which meant the soldiers had permission to run wild, seize, loot, burn, kill, and plunder. Pirates, as well as armies, were famous (or rather infamous) for the **havoc** they caused.

Rolled his Rs: In some languages, Rs are often or sometimes "rolled," so that the R comes out of the mouth vibrating over the flip of the tongue's tip against the lower teeth. The Scots take a certain pride in this manifestation of their Scottishness, and the Scots of western Scotland particularly do so. A young Scottish friend of mine in fact told me that in general the Scots of eastern Scotland do NOT roll their Rs, and are therefore very slightly looked down upon by the Scots of western Scotland. Ayrshire, of course, is in *western* Scotland, and we can assume, accordingly, that Robert Burns rolled his Rs right mightily, just like my friend, who, come to think of it, looks remarkably like Burns himself.

Conjure: To summon up, as with an oath or magic spell. A magician is a **conjurer.** There are many little phrases that we commonly use, almost like incantations, preliminary to performing some act. I suppose we think that doing so will bring luck to the action. The phrase "Once upon a time," which so famously begins so many "nursery" stories, immediately casts the listener into a magical moment of long ago, **conjuring up** in the imagination goblins and giants, Princes and Princesses, gnomes, trolls, fairies and all the wonderful rest. Why do I recall, for no one ever uses the term now, the phrase, once used almost as an oath, "By the great horned spoon"? What was a "horned spoon," and how could it, once called upon, conjure up whatever help one might need to complete an endeavor?

Offal (OFF-ul): The entrails (intestines and so forth) of a butchered animal. In Scotland the national dish is "haggis," a sort of pudding made out of a sheep's entrails. Since most people with lesser stomachs would rather not eat entrails, the word **offal** also means "waste," "rubbish," or something rather disgusting to be thrown aside. I have, myself, eaten a bit of haggis here and there, and in fact it was not bad at all, rather like meatloaf. I think it would have been quite good with ketchup, but none was available, and anyway the Scots would be horrified, and their feelings hurt, if you actually put *ketchup* on their National Dish. Often, by the way, when I use the word **offal** I put "awful" in front of it, which may be fun for you too. (Hint: Never, *ever,* exclaim to your Mom at dinner that it tastes like **awful offal!**)

Borne: This is the past participle of the verb "to bear," as in "to carry." I used "borne" here, rather than "carry," because it sounds more fancy and high-fallutin', which every haggis aspires to being, naturally.

Addressed: Of course no one actually addresses, or speaks to, a haggis. You generally speak to what can speak back to you, and no haggis has ever actually spoken, any more than a meatloaf might. But an **address**, aside from what you put on an envelope, is also a formal manner of presenting oneself. For example, when a gentleman is paying courtship to a lady, he is **addressing** her attention. In this case it is the haggis that is being formally courted and paid high respect.

Wee libation: **Wee**, as you know, means "little" in the Scottish dialect. ("Wee-wee" is something else of course, and not just in Scotland.) A **libation** in ancient times was the act of pouring out some wine or oil during the course of a sacrifice to the gods. It has now come to mean, in good humor, an alcoholic beverage, which you excuse yourself for drinking by implying that you are drinking to the honor of some god. Certainly you are honoring Bacchus, the God of Wine and Drink. A **wee libation** might actually mean a "stiff drink," but the "wee" helps you to pretend that it is less than it is!

Decorous: See "Decorum" under Dryden.

Bonnie: Someone or something pretty or pleasant to look at, as in a "bonnie (or bonny) lassie."

Braw: Anything that is fine or excellent, as in a **braw** day. It is a Scots form of "brave."

Idiom: This is from the Greek word *idioma,* meaning a peculiarity or a peculiar phrase. In language it is commonly associated with the special dialect of a people, region, or class. Middle Schoolers have their own **idiomatic** way of speaking that is somewhat different from that of a college student, a parent, or a professor. The "South" speaks with an **idiom** very different from that of a New Englander. Even in the South there are **idiomatic** distinctions between "Cajuns," "Appalachians," Alabamans, "Eubonics," and even "Red Necks." Professor Higgins, in "My Fair Lady," could tell exactly where anybody lived in England just by listening to the **idioms** of their speech. Sir Winston Churchill was reputed to be able to do almost the same, in real life.

Diction: Well, tell me. What is a "dictionary"? **Diction** defines your choice of words and manner of speaking them. Some people are said to have "good **diction**" and others not so good. A dictionary, of course, has nothing to do with how you use the words you know, but it contains the raw material, all the words that you must choose from if you are to have any **diction** at all. **Diction** comes from the Latin word *dicere*, which means "to speak, to say." The first real dictionary was compiled by Samuel Johnson. He published his great work in London in 1757, and was famous not only for his dictionary, but for his **diction** too! He became even more famous when his friend, Boswell, wrote his greatly acclaimed biography, *The Life of Johnson,* which remains a model for all writers of biography.

WORDSWORTH

Madame La Guillotine: Who has not heard of the **guillotine**? Beyond that, why "**Madame**"? Well, one supposes that such a "humane" device, for it was devised to be more quick and efficient in its work than a mere axe man's blade, which could readily miss the neck in the excitement of performing the blow. The **guillotine** might be considered a more graceful, and therefore feminine, way to kill someone off. Besides, the word for "death" in French, *la morte,* is also feminine. In any case, forms of the **guillotine** had been around since the 13th century, but Dr. Joseph-Ignace Guillotin, just after the French Revolution in July, 1789, proposed that the enemies of the state should be executed by this device for the sake of both its efficiency and humaneness. Over 40,000 people of all classes, but mostly aristocrats such as the former King himself, and his Queen, Marie Antoinette, were publicly killed by it before jeering crowds in the two years following its first use in 1792. It took 2/100ths of a second for the head to be severed, and many were of the opinion that the head itself retained consciousness for up to 20 to 30 seconds. Its last use was in France in 1977.

Excesses: **Excess** comes from the Latin word, *excedere,* to go beyond. Anything "in **excess**," or **excessive**, goes beyond the normal limits. This can be bad, as in "the use of **excessive** force," or as in someone's being "**excessively** lazy." An extreme amount of good can also be bad, as when someone may be "**excessively** studious." Among the **excesses** of the French Revolution was the tremendous slaughter of so many people by Madame La Guillotine. The period in French history between 1792 and 1794 came to be known as "The Terror."

Amidst: simply means "in the middle of," which we maybe more often tend to say. But **amidst** is quite pleasant, I think, and so I use it. You can also say "in the midst," as in "the boy stands in the midst of the herd of buffaloes."

Etched: The past participle of the verb **to etch**, which comes from a German word meaning to corrode or eat. An **etching** is usually an artwork in which lines are created on metal or glass

80

by the action of an acid. It is technically a rather complicated process, but can create beautiful and dramatic works of art. The phrase "come up and see my **etchings**" entered into use as a result of the attraction etchings apparently had, once upon a time, on the sensibilities of young ladies. A young man, who might not have even owned an **etching**, might claim to do so, and invite a trusting young lady to visit his apartment, but for amorous rather than artistic purposes. Art, and even poetry, can be put to sly use.

Cataclysms: Tremendous down-pourings of water, or violent acts of nature such as earthquakes, that cause tremendous damage. The word comes from the Greek, *kata* meaning "down," and *klysein*, to wash. War is often described as a **cataclysm**. What is a "catastrophe"? (Hint: *Strophe* in Greek means a "turning.")

BYRON

Swoon: An old-fashioned term meaning "to faint." But maybe there is a slight difference between the two. In my own mind, "fainting" means you fall down flat and hard and without any fuss. When one **swoons**, on the other hand, the **swooner** almost has to be a lady, who sort of gently, gracefully, and rather elegantly loses consciousness, and lands perfectly on a chair or sofa looking beautiful.

Smelling salts: A mixture of carbonate of ammonium (ammonia) and usually some fragrant scent, held under the nose of someone who has swooned. If you have ever smelled ammonia up close, you know that it jerks you "awake" pretty quick. A Victorian lady who was subject to fainting spells, perhaps because her corset was too tight, might even wear a pin or brooch, which contained some smelling salts in case of a sudden swooning. In the 1960s young ladies swooned not because of tight corsets, but over "Rock Stars." Nowadays almost no one swoons, and **smelling salts** are past history. If someone does faint, the best treatment is simply to have them lie down, and elevate their feet. In Victorian times, of course, such a maneuver would have been thought highly unseemly, and not actually to be performed on a lady because it might betray etiquette by revealing her ankles.

Deplore: From the Latin *deplorare*, this means "to weep bitterly, lament, mourn." **To deplore** something is to express disapproval of it, as when a Mom might say "I **deplore** the terrible mess in your room," or "You simply cannot keep an elephant in your room! It will create a **deplorable** mess!"

Seduced: To **seduce** is to lead on by smooth talk and manner, to tempt someone into doing something they might not really want to do, but which the **seducer** makes out to sound marvelous and fun. For ages past, of course, men have been seducing ladies into this and that, and vice-versa, too. Sometimes **seduction**, as by Casanova, the famous lover in the 18th century, almost reaches to the heights of art.

Supercalafragilisticexpialadocious: Exactly what it sounds like, Greater than Great, an invented word that you will recall from Mary Poppins, a wonderful book and film.

Harrow: A boys' school in England, founded in 1572 by Queen Elizabeth I, which along with Eton and Winchester is very famous for the prestige of its name, the quality of its traditions, and the excellence of the education it provides. Your own school does all of the above too, but has not been around for quite so long a time.

Travelling: Exactly the same as **traveling**, only with two Ls. The English double the L, but we Americans more economically use just one L. Because Byron was English, I have used two

LLs, but sometimes I do it anyway, if I want to emphasize the fact that the trip will be Llong, and I am truly going to do some realll travellllling. Sometimes I double it just because I want to. Sometimes I don't double it because I feel a little weak.

Hellespont (as in **The Hellespont**): Please raise your hand if you know where this place is. I think that 24% of you know. You may remember it from geography or from reading Homer's *Iliad*. Troy was located very near the **Hellespont**, that narrow (but still pretty wide for swimming) body of water that connects the Black Sea with the Aegean Sea, which is part of the Mediterranean Sea, which is surrounded by—what? Name five countries that border on the Mediterranean Sea:

1.)_____
2.)_____
3.)_____
4.)_____
5.)_____.

Brigands: Thieves, outlaws, and cutthroats, often hiding out in hills and forests where they lie in wait for unwary travelers, pouncing upon them to rob or kidnap them, and then leaving them destitute if not dead. Bands of **brigands** presented a great risk to people traveling in Byron's day in Greece, but even so the idea of the **brigand** was rather romanticized into an image of a bold character beyond the law, who led a wild, free life.

Ottoman Turks: Before the First World War in 1914, the Turkish (**Ottoman**) Empire dominated large areas of what we now call "The Middle East," as well as Egypt. Because Turkey was on the "losing side" in that war, the **Ottoman** Empire was broken up, and Turkey was set on the road to becoming the modern, democratic nation it is today. But during the period of the **Ottoman Empire**, which lasted from 1517 to 1918, the Turkish rulers of those countries, although wealthy, were barbarously despotic and cruel. By 1918 the Ottoman Empire had become so weakened by poor administration that it was ripe for collapse.

SHELLEY

Archetypal (ARK-uh-TYPE-ul): The original, the most perfect pattern on which lesser copies may be based. In this case, the word describes Shelley as being the best, the greatest example of our idea of a "Romantic Poet," just as one might say that Robert Louis Stevenson's *Treasure Island* is the **archetypal** pirate story, or Superman the **archetypal** super-hero, or even Bugs Bunny the **archetypal** funny rabbit.

Elegy: You already know this one. Please, I beg you, refer back to Thomas Gray and "The Elegy in a Country Churchyard."

COLERIDGE.

The Rhyme of the Ancient Mariner: Of course you may not have heard of this poem. Why should you? And, by the way, who, and what, is a "mariner"? Doubtless you know THAT one! Anyway, a mariner is a seaman, a sailor, the term deriving from the Latin for "the sea," which is *mare*, with the "e" on the end pronounced like an A, and a "long" one at that. It is NOT pronounced like a "mare," as for example when you mean a lady horse. In any case, "The Rhyme of the Ancient Mariner" is about a seaman who kills an albatross, a bird of good omen, in the distant reaches of a cold, cold ocean, and for the act is condemned to wander the oceans forever in his ghostly ship, crossing and recrossing that cold and merciless sea.

Albatross: A wonderful big bird, long a sight and symbol loved by sailors for its size and strength. The albatross in flight is beautiful, stretching out its wings with such an ability to catch every current of wind that it can stay in the air for days at a time, and has been known to fly non-stop around the earth. No wonder that in the days of sailing ships, whose sails act as "wings" themselves, this majestic creature was looked upon with awe and reverence by the sailors who saw it.

Kubla Khan: A Chinese emperor, whose name can also be spelled **Khubilai Khan**. He was born in 1214 more or less, and was a descendant of the great Genghis Khan, who had so ruthlessly and effectively run around conquering Asia before him. **Kubla** tried to do more of the same, but with less effect, and spent a great deal of his Imperial money building a fabulous city, which in his poem Coleridge poetically imagines. Alph is the name of a river in Greece that actually does run suddenly into, and then under, the ground.

Christabel: This is another poem by Coleridge, written in much the same style as "Kubla Khan," about a lady vampire. She is beautiful but deadly, like Nature herself in the Romantic poet's world, and you had better be careful around her, as with any vampire. Just as in "vampire movies" today, lady vampires are invariably gorgeous creatures. Coleridge was the first to present one so, but of course in poetry, which people read more of in his day than they do today since there were no movies.

Romantic Poets: When a poet is described as being **Romantic**, it does not mean he or she is necessarily a practitioner of the art of "romantic love." A **Romantic** poet is, however, in love with a lot of stuff: the power of nature, the power of beauty, the power of individual freedom. The world, the **Romantic Poets** thought, is a huge place in a huge universe that is both beautiful and cruel at once, maybe like Christabel. The world and all natural things can fill you with rapture, and at the same time kill you. The **Romantic Poets**, Shelley, Coleridge, Wordsworth, Byron, and Keats, seized upon this concept, and what they made of it in their poetry very much influences our own thoughts about nature to this day.

Stupors: What is a **stupor**? You can certainly be in a **stupor** without being "stupid." It is any state in which the mind or the senses are dulled. A person who uses drugs or too much alcohol may fall into a **stupor**. And if they have really overdosed the next step is that they go into a coma. And after a coma there is death, which is (of course!) the ultimate **stupor**.

Lurks: Of course you know what "lurks" means, and I scarcely know why I include it here. It means sort of slyly "hanging about," watching maybe, and perhaps without an altogether good purpose. When I am eating a bit of junk food from time to time, our dogs, and much more rarely our cats, **lurk** about, hoping we will accidentally drop some titbit into their mouths, or maybe a whole steak, in which case they would think they had died and gone to Heaven.

KEATS

Countenance: Aha! Here is a word for you. It means not only just your "face" and its features (nose, eyes, mouth, and so forth, including maybe even the zits, which do not bear discussion here) but your expression, too. It comes from the Latin verb, *continere*, which means "to hold together." Old French took the Latin and applied it to the face, and how all of one's facial parts "held together," for good or bad, mean or sad, suggesting not only the actual appearance of "the features," but also their behavior. This sense of whether or not your "features" are behaving themselves decently, holding themselves back rather than sticking your tongue out and turning up your nose at every passerby, gave the word a positive meaning. Thus the verb **to countenance** means also to give approval. Your teacher will **countenance** the fact that you do not wiggle your ears at her, turning your pleasing **countenance** ridiculous.

POE

Longfellow: **Henry Wadsworth Longfellow** was a very famous American poet (1807-1882), who had a wonderful white beard, and lived in a lovely house in Cambridge, Massachusetts, very near the campus of Harvard University. His house has been preserved as an historical site, and you can visit it if you go to Harvard, or even if you don't go to Harvard.

TENNYSON

Reviled: Regarded or treated as vile. Anything vile, of course, is disgusting, wicked, hateful, repulsive, cheap, or even simply terribly inferior. Do not taste bile: it is very, very vile. On the other hand, be slow to **revile** a poet. He, or she, may be much better than you think. Poe, so much **reviled** in his own time, has now become a poetic Super Hero.

Brows: Of course you have two of these on your face. The word **brow** comes from the Sanskrit *bhru*, meaning "eyebrow," and middle English *bruwe*, meaning the same. Your **brows** are right at the edge of the jumping off point where the forehead curves suddenly into the eye socket, but also in a more general way they can include some nearby forehead also. Whether or not you have a pleasing countenance much depends on whether you are contracting your **brows** using the *frontalis* and *corrugator* muscles, which draw the brows together in a frown, or not. And don't forget that hills and cliffs have **brows** too, where you can stand on the height gazing at a distant horizon. Ships, by the way, do NOT have **brows**, but a ship does have a "prow," where you can stand high on its bow, or even climb out on the bowsprit, to gaze at the watery horizon.

Ulysses: Have we not done him already? You all know his story, ten years in the making, coming home from Troy, and all that. And you know also that the Romans called him Odysseus, which is why we call Homer's great poetic tale *The Odyssey*.

Lotus Eaters: The Lotus Eaters is a poem published by Tennyson in 1831, but based on the episode in *The Odyssey* when Odysseus and his men find themselves in the land of the *lotophagi*. "Loto" means "the lotus fruit" in Greek, and "phagi" means to eat. Those who ate of the lotus lost all desire to return home. Tennyson's poem describes, in rich and sensuous language, the temptation to abandon the world of active struggle and creation, and instead embrace a passive, drugged, "out-of-it" existence, where all is forgotten. Odysseus, being strong, of course overcame this temptation, which he could in no way countenance despite its seductive appeal.

Lofty: Very high. Elevated. Exalted. Eminent. It derives from the German word *luft*, meaning "air." When you "go aloft" you go up in the air. A "hayloft" is where? In the bottom of the barn or up high in the top? And, yes, you could even have a "**lofty** countenance," but some people might think you were also stuck up, with your nose so high in the air.

Modred: I believe **Modred** has been in a lot of movies. He is always the bad guy. His armor and horse are invariably black. He is the leader of all those Barons and Earls who wanted to destroy the goodly fellowship and lofty principles of King Arthur, Camelot, and the Knights of the Round Table. He plots and plans, consumed with jealousy. And finally, in "that last weird battle in the west," as Tennyson introduces it in his poem,

> . . . **Modred** smote his liege
> Hard on that helm which many a heathen sword
> Had beaten thin; while Arthur at one blow,
> Striking the last stroke with Excalibur,
> Slew him, and, all but slain himself, he fell.

DICKINSON

Quirky: Surprising, unexpected, from the Old Norse, *querk*, which was that part of a bird's neck that we call its crop, which takes a sudden twist or turn. A flourish in writing, where a sudden curving turn occurs, is called a **quirk**. Therefore anything **quirky** is unexpected, unpredictable, and unusual too. Emily Dickinson's poetry was certainly all of this, and even within her poems themselves sudden little "turns" occurred. Her poems still verbally astonish and surprise us. In her own day she seemed even more **quirky**, because people were not used to such liberties and flourishes, to the point of astonishments, being taken with the accepted forms of poetic diction.

Perimeter (pe-RIM-uh-ter): *Peri* in Greek means "around." Therefore a "Periscope," which tacks on the Greek *skopein*, to see, is what? It is, literally, a "look around" device, useful to sub(under)mariners(sailors of the *mare*, sea). *Metron* in Greek is "to measure," from which we also get the term "meter," which is a bit longer than a yard. Accordingly the **perimeter** of anything is the length or measurement around it. It can also mean a line, like a fence, around some area of land. It can even have a behavioral implication, as for example if you are told that "you should always stay within the **perimeters** of good manners."

Concise: Brief, to the point, of few words. When they talk, some people are **concise**, and some are "logodaedalian." Now there, again, is a fine word indeed! "Logo" means "word" in Greek. And do you remember the myth of Daedalus? Daedalus made himself wings, the feathers stuck together with wax, with which he determined to fly up to the sun. His father cautioned him against such a rash act, but Daedalus was (after all!) a teen-ager, and decided to fly up there anyway. When he did, the wax melted due to the sun's heat, his wings came apart, and he fell like a stone to his death in the sea. And so, the opposite of concise is "logodaedalian," which means you use words in soaring flights of fancy, carrying you higher and even higher on their wings, until all of a sudden, at the lofty height of what you thought you were saying, you suddenly discover you do not even understand yourself. And so, sadly, you fall into a sea of confusion, the idea you were trying to express lost in a welter of melted words.

WHITMAN

Cloistered: A **cloister** is a quiet space, maybe a walled garden, often associated with a church or monastery, where one can go to meditate, think, or pray. It is a place to which you can more or less "escape," the very opposite of, for example, a big shopping mall, or the intersection between the two very biggest streets in your town or city. Can you name those streets? Have you ever been in a **cloister**?

Microcosm: Think. You know what this means, because you know what "cosmic" means, as in "the cosmic force" or "cosmic rays" or "cosmology," the study of the universe. Anything "cosmic" is humongous, like the universe. But then "micro" means, as you know, tiny tiny, as in "microscope." So what is a "microcosm"? What is a tiny universe? Someone once said that within a grain of sand there lies a universe. Within Emily Dickinson's tiny garden was enough for her to discover a whole universe of meaning. So remember, the littlest things can contain a lot, a cosmic lot. They are **microcosmic**.

Correspondence: Of course you see that in this word lies the word "respond." And naturally a response means you are replying to something someone may have said or asked. The "*co-*" means "with," indicating that two people are going back and forth, just as when they "cooperate" and are accordingly "operating" with each other. In any case, **correspondence** used to be thought of as mostly mail, letters written back and forth between two friends, and of course e-mail is simply **correspondence** through cyberspace. If two drummers drum back and forth to each other, that is also **corresponding**, and I suppose equally through cyberspace, or at least "space."

LEAR

Limericks: A **limerick** is a nonsense poem, wherein the first, second, and fifth lines rhyme, and also the second and third. Some nonsense person who lived in Limerick, a town in Ireland, must have used this form with happy effect, and thence it derives its name. But it was Edward Lear who really made it popular. Here is one of Lear's **limericks**:

> There was an old man who said "Hush!
> I perceive a young bird in this bush."
>   When they said, "Is it small?"
>   He replied , "Not at all!
> It is four times as big as the bush."

Doggerel: A piece of **doggerel** usually comes in the form of a trivial, comic bit of verse; a "jingle." Because it is so silly, it is not dignified with the name "poetry," any more than "pig Latin," or what is also called "dog latin" is really Latin. Therefore, one imagines, the "dog" in **doggerel**. I suppose such verse could have been called "piggerel" too, but who knows how words sort themselves out? Or how anything else does either.

Whimsy: An odd, fanciful, curious notion that is usually rather playful as well. For example, I have, myself, the **whimsical** idea that someday I am going to possess a huge bird suit, rather like Big Bird's, with feathers and a great lovely beak, and sit on top of our house. So far my wife will not let me. And, by the way, **whimsy** can also be properly spelled **whimsey**, which IS rather **whimsical** of it.

Risible: comes from the Latin word *ridere*, which means "to laugh," or to be inclined to laughter. You might astonish your teacher some day, if she is inclined to humor and has said something funny, to pay her the compliment of observing how much you enjoyed her "**risible** remark."

Runcible: This word was made famous by Lear when he wrote of the "**runcible** spoon" in "The Owl and the Pussy Cat." A **runcible** is a sort of fork, with two broad prongs and another long curving one, and who knows what you did with it? A "**runcible** spoon," one imagines, is a combination fork and spoon, quite handy for stabbing peas and souping soup.

Rollicking: This implies that whatever one is doing is being done in a carefree, gay, lively, and funny manner. Every now and then one likes to have (don't you?) a "**rollicking** good time" or even a "frolicking **rollick**."

YEATS

Renowned: Someone who is **renowned** is famous, or even infamous, which is "famous" in a bad way. A person can be **renowned**, but so also can a place, for example: "the moon is **renowned** for being made of cheese" "The cow is **renowned** for jumping over the moon." You may even be **renowned** among your classmates, or certainly your teachers, for being an excellent student, which does not mean you necessarily have to get great grades all the time, but that you try hard, work hard, and speak up in class. (I will now whisper to you the secret of success in class and elsewhere: it is "<u>don't be afraid</u>.")

Lady Gregory of Coole: Born Isabella Augusta Persse in 1852 of an old Irish family, she married Sir William Gregory when she was 28. She lived happily with Sir William in his ancestral home, one of the great country houses of that part of Ireland, called Coole Park. There, after Sir William's death, she entertained and promoted numerous aspiring Irish authors and playwrights, such as Yeats and George Moore, who became very important in bringing back to life Irish culture, long suppressed by the English. She and Yeats gave life and vitality to the "Abbey Theater" in Dublin, which famously promoted these values, leading Irish and in fact English literature into a new modernity.

Subjugated: To **subjugate** is easily remembered because it is so much like "to subdue." When you **subjugate**, or subdue, anything, you overcome it, defeat it, beat it down. We would like to **subjugate** Terrorism.

Renaissance: Rebirth (from the French word "naissance," birth). Do you know when or what "the" **Renaissance** was? It was that time in history, in the 14th, 15th, and 16th centuries, when there was a great revival of learning after the "dark ages" that followed the fall of the Roman Empire. The **Renaissance** was a rebirth of interest in art, literature, and learning, which began in Italy, and spread throughout Europe. The **Renaissance** was an exciting time when the cultures of classical Greece and Rome were rediscovered, and it led to our own civilization's becoming the rich mixture of cultures that it is today. In Ireland, the **Renaissance** was marked by the efforts of Yeats and Lady Gregory to bring back and reawaken an appreciation for the cultural heritage of that island. They succeeded brilliantly.

Leprechauns: These are particularly Irish little creatures, who take the form of little old men who can lead you to treasure. Ireland, having been for so long (but no longer) such a poor country, the only wealth its people could imagine was the wealth of wishful thinking, and the hope that one might meet a **Leprechaun** who would lead one to a pot of gold. Nowadays we buy lottery tickets with the same hope in mind, but our chances of winning the "big pot" are about the same as our chances of meeting a **Leprechaun**.

Innisfree: A place in Ireland that is almost more imagined than real. As the poem implies, it is a place remote and beautiful, quiet and far from the sound and strife of bustling cities. It is a place that Yeats, through this poem, endowed with a great deal of Romantic meaning to any Irish ear that might hear of "going to **Innisfree**," just as in America Thoreau gave such a meaning to "Walden Pond." If you tend to like things Irish, and would like to see, if you have not seen it already, a delightful film about Ireland, you should rent "The Quiet Man." It takes place in Ireland about 75 years ago, and stars John Wayne in a role that is my favorite of all his many films. In it, if you listen for it, you will hear mentioned the village of **Innisfree**. The very word sets you, and the film, in the heart of a most beautiful part of that beautiful Island.

POUND

Freud: **Sigmund Freud** (1856-1939) almost "invented" modern psychotherapy. He is responsible for that image we so often see of the psychiatrist sitting by a sofa on which a patient is stretched out, eyes closed, engaged in dredging up some dim, subconscious memory, long suppressed. **Freud** taught us that in the depths of one's "unconscious" self lay experiences that profoundly affected behavior. His technique, which became the "classic" method of treatment for many psychiatric conditions, was to probe deeply into the patient's memory, reveal the experience that was causing mental pain, and by revealing it come both to understand it and resolve it.

Picasso: Just as Freud almost "invented" modern psychotherapy, **Pablo Picasso** (1881-1973) almost "invented" modern art. Before **Picasso**, painters had mostly painted pretty scenes, true to nature. **Picasso** took nature apart in somewhat the same way as Freud took the mind apart. His curious but interesting distortions of reality (as our eyes normally perceive reality) dominated modern art throughout the 20ᵗʰ century. Both Freud and **Picasso** showed us that "things are not necessarily what they seem." What do you think? Is the sky blue? Or can it be green, or yellow, or red?

Einstein: Even more than Picasso, **Albert Einstein** (1879-1955) fractured our perception of reality. At the very same time as Freud and Picasso were doing their great work, at the beginning of the 20ᵗʰ century, **Einstein** came out with his famous "Theory of Relativity," which shattered and expanded our perception and understanding of the whole universe. Before **Einstein** it was thought that the universe was a predictable place where one plus one always had to equal two. **Einstein's** work demonstrated mathematically that this is not necessarily true, and that everything, including time and space, is relative to where you stand as the observer: the place of perception. The only absolute was the speed of light (186,000 miles a second). But now physicists are beginning to challenge even that "absolute." Who knows what is what? We cannot get into the "mind" of a quark, or the speed of light, can we? And does anyone know what a "quark" is? Given the theories of **Einstein** could it be that there is not much difference between a "Quark" and a "Quack"?

Moths: Moths, of course, are famously attracted to light, and perfectly willing to burn themselves up for the thrill of "being lit."

Ardor: Intense heat, as mostly felt in the emotions. **Ardor** is a somewhat more poetic word than "passion." A lover might say, particularly if you were wearing a cape and possessed a certain panache and therefore had a great feather in your cap, "My heart burns with ardor at the very sight of your beautiful little finger." The adjective is **ardent**, as in "he was an **ardent** fisherman, even though he never caught a fish."

Legacy: An inheritance, that is, the property or money that comes down to one through the will of someone who has died. It is also whatever else comes down to us from the past. We are the **legatees** of the past. Burns left Scotland the rich heritage of his poetry, which **legacy** the Scots take great pride in both honoring and protecting.

Enamored: In Latin *Amor* means "love"; in French it is *Amour*; in Italian *Amore*; in Spanish

Amar. What do you think, then, that "In **amore**" means? Quite so. It means "to be in love with," or at least to be very fetched by. Of course you can be **enamored** of your dog, too. Or **enamored** of fishing. Or even **enamored** of thumbing through glossaries, although this is carrying the definition a little far.

Mussolini: **Benito Mussolini** (1883-1945) was the archetypal dictator, or tyrant, who forcibly came to power in Italy in 1922, and ruled that nation with an iron hand. He established a pattern of dictatorship called "Fascism," which was much admired by Hitler. The basic techniques were based on threats and fear. Hitler copied his methods, and brought them to an even greater degree of "perfection" and ruthlessness.

Cantos: A **canto** is a part or division of a (usually long) poem. It comes from the Italian verb for "to sing," *cantare.* The most famous series of **Cantos** were those written by Dante, the great Italian poet, comparable in his scope to Shakespeare, in the 14th century. His cantos were called "The Divine Comedy," and they describe in rich, poetic detail Dante's vision of the universe. He described "Hell" in "The Inferno"; "Purgatory," which is between Heaven and Hell; and "Paradise," which is Heaven. Each realm was given 33 **Cantos**, which acted as chapters do in a book of prose. *The Divine Comedy* is one of the great creations within the cultural heritage of the western world. And, no, it is not funny. It is called a "comedy" because in Italian *commedia* has a somewhat broader meaning than simply something that causes us to laugh. It includes more generally all sorts of play-acting. We are the actors, dwelling between Heaven and Hell, in a play produced by the Divine Creator, the Maestro of the universe. Dante, interestingly, did not himself give to his poem the name, *La Divina Commedia.* That name was given to it its admirers after his death.

ELIOT

Erudition (air-you-DISH-un): Scholarship, learning, the knowledge gained by study and reading, mostly applied to literature, history, and the arts. A great professor who has written great books on some subject to which he has devoted much thought and study would be said to be **erudite**, and his **erudition** would be much admired.

Ultimately: *Ultima* in Latin means the end, the most remote place, beyond which it is impossible to go farther. An "ultima," by the way, is also the last syllable of a word. In ancient times, the Greeks and Romans thought that *Thule* was the farthest, most northern place in the world. *Ultima Thule* must have therefore been on the outskirts of Thule, even farther north than "downtown" *Thule* itself. There was no *Ultima Ultima Thule*, nor can you go farther north than the north North Pole. Ultima and **ultimately** therefore mean "finally," as in "I will **ultimately** clean up my room, Mom, which I am sorry is such a deplorable mess." To which remark she might reply, "If you don't, I am going to send you to *Ultima Thule!*" Now, can you tell me what an "ultimatum" is?

Michelangelo: It may be difficult not to know who **Michelangelo** was, but it is possible that one might not know his middle name, which was "Buonarroti." But just **Michelangelo** will quite do. After all, **Michelangelo** (1475-1564) is the greatest and most famous of all the great painters and sculptors of the Renaissance, and stands in the world of art as high as Shakespeare and Dante do in the world of literature. Perhaps his most famous work was the painting on the ceiling of the Sistine Chapel in Rome. Before **Michelangelo** was commissioned by the Pope to paint it, it was simply a rather dull ceiling way up in the air with some stars stuck on it. Even the scaffold, which **Michelangelo** also designed, was an engineering work of art.. Month in and month out, year in and year out, **Michelangelo** climbed up, and, lying on his aching back, he painted for hours by the light of a candle. The Sistine Chapel ceiling was a miracle of effort and genius. Go to Rome and see it.

WORLD WAR ONE POETS

Napoleon: Born into a Corsican family of some ambition, and gifted with tremendous energy, **Napoleon Bonaparte** (1769-1821) rose to become the Emperor of France and one of the most famous military leaders in all history. Like Hitler 125 years later, he conquered almost all of Europe, but then he had to make a disastrous retreat from Moscow in 1812. He ultimately "met his Waterloo" near the little village of, yes, Waterloo, in Belgium, defeated by forces led by the English Duke of Wellington. He was captured and exiled to the tiny island of St. Helena, a speck of land far from Europe in the south Atlantic Ocean. There he died. Some said he was poisoned by the British, but in fact he probably had a cancer of the stomach. Have you ever seen a picture of **Napoleon,** with his hand stuck between the buttons of his greatcoat over his stomach? Maybe he had a stomachache even when the picture was being painted. As for his losing the battle of Waterloo, even the Duke of Wellington said it was "a near run thing," meaning that the outcome might easily have been an English defeat. Some even say that **Napoleon,** who was suffering that day from a painful bottom due to hemorrhoids, could not sit on his horse, and that if he had been able to gallop about leading his troops, he might well have been victorious. It is on such small and indelicate things that history sometimes turns. By the way, where is Corsica?

Depleted: Emptied, from the Latin *deplere*. Anything that is **depleted** has been exhausted, drained dry. World War One, in which so many millions were killed, not only **depleted** the world of those individuals and their talents, but also left the world **depleted** of former values and even its hopes for future progress.

Cynicism: Originally, in ancient Greece, the **Cynics** were a sect of philosophers who held to the belief that strict virtue, rejecting worldly needs and pleasures, was the only good. Holding this belief, they embraced the temptation to criticize others in society who they thought were not as virtuous as themselves. A **cynic** is therefore now thought of as a person who thinks that people's apparently "good" motives and actions are only the result of selfishness. A **cynic** tends to scorn and mock the beliefs and actions of others. A **cynic** is, as a result, not much fun to be around.

Ypres (ee-PRAY): A little village in Belgium, once famous for its lace. Now, because of the terrible and bloody battles fought near **Ypres** by the English in World War One, its name has become, along with that of Verdun, the Somme, and the Argonne, representative of the horrors of the mud and slaughter that occurred in the trenches of that war.

MARQUIS

Pinnacle: In architecture, this is the little cap or turret that rises above the roof of a building. Any peaky point on the top of anything else is therefore a **pinnacle**. It is the very tippy-top, where few people might be able to climb. Dante, Chaucer, Shakespeare, Milton, and Eliot stand on the **pinnacle** of the western literary mountain, with all the other writers, greater or less, spilling down the slope. How far up towards the **pinnacle** would you put the author of *Tom Sawyer*? In the blank space provided please fill in the name of the author who wrote *Tom Sawyer*.

Brash: This word may come from a Scottish dialect, incorporating the idea of rash, dash, clash, bash, and maybe even mash. It describes any action, or person, who is hasty, impudent, probably thoughtless, and rather rude. A **brash** person does not care if he clashes, bashes, mashes, or dashes. Would you like to be a **brash** person? Or not?

Bawdy: A **bawdy** person may not necessarily be brash, but probably is. **Bawdy** people tend to bash about in a quite brash manner, making a lot of indecent gestures and noises, disturbing everyone else, and generally acting in a low and nasty manner. They will probably end up getting drunk, and vomiting all over the furniture, until they finally pass out and sleep it off. This is, in any case, my definition, and if you want more particular specifics you will have to go to your own dictionary.

Prohibition: In 1919, finally giving in to the outcries of a minority of people who wanted to make alcoholic beverages illegal, the United States government passed the Volstead Act, which did just that. Immediately everyone began drinking more than ever, getting liquor from bootleggers or even making what was called "bathtub gin," which could quite blind you. A whole criminal industry sprang up, which smuggled liquor into this country, where it was sold or served in hideaway nightclubs called "speakeasies." A famous smuggler was a man named "McCoy," who illegally brought to this country some of the famous whiskies and wines from Europe and Britain. A good whiskey accordingly came to be called "the real McCoy," a term still in use when you want to say that something is "the real thing." The Volstead act, a highly unsuccessful social experiment, ultimately failed miserably, and was repealed in 1933.

CUMMINGS

Mannerism: Any method of painting, writing, or sculpting that assumes the style, or "manner," of a preceding style, but adapts it to the artist's needs at his present moment in time. Pope took Dryden's method and imposed on it his own more rigid rules and method. Creative though he or she may be, the **mannerist** runs the risk of being a little dull, being basically a sort of "copy-cat."

Cubists: All right, what is a cube? Quick, how many sides does it have? Would all the sides be of equal area? Of equal shape? What would a cube look like if one side was 2 inches by 2 inches, and the other was 4.4 by 7.2 inches? Would it be a cube at all? Well, not ordinarily, but sometimes, and particularly in your imagination, the "ordinary" can suddenly become "extraordinary," as in a dream. Or in the mind of an artist, who might put into paint, or sculpture, or even poetry a reinterpretation of the world. Painters such as Picasso started doing this sort of thing in the 1910s or thereabouts. In their imagination they broke the world we ordinarily see into little fragments, like "cubes," and put that vision of it on canvas. These artists were asking us to rethink how we see the world, telling us that there may be other realities that our eyes have not recognized. The world may not be, they "said" in their paintings, what it seems. A famous **cubist** painting by Marcel DuChamp is the "Nude Descending a Staircase."

Dadaists (DAH-dah-ists): Not to be outdone, after the cubists had fractured our perception of "reality," the **Dadaists** came along and in their paintings and poetry fractured it even further. They made reality sometimes look even silly, but reality certainly can be as "silly" as it can be tragic. Their artistic ideas were not only astonishing, but also very powerful and thought provoking. A famous **Dada** image was a fur-lined teacup. They also showed that ordinary objects in the right setting might be 'perfectly well viewed as "works of art," such as an ordinary toilet. What do you think of such "art"?

Depict: To show or illustrate, as in, for example, "see DE PICTure."

Dissonances (DISS-o-nan-ses): "*Sonus*" in Latin means sound. The "Dis" part acts as a negative. When you DISagree with someone you are NOT agreeing. I think that in modern slang you can use the DIS part all alone, as when someone gets "dissed." In any case, pretty clearly, a dissonance is a harsh sound, not in keeping with the sound you might expect. Just as painters gave us a new insight into the world by fracturing it into its component parts, so also did composers begin to fracture the usually accepted harmonies of music. As wars DISrupt the peace, causing DISmay and DIStress, the **dissonances** that now became popular in musical composition produced a DIScord that sometimes shocked people's ears and demanded their attention.

Comprehensible: Comes from the Latin world, *comprehendere*, meaning "to seize, lay hold of, grasp." In our use of the word, either as the noun **comprehension**, or the verb **to comprehend**, or the adjective **comprehensible**, the meaning generally relates to "understanding." In other words, you "seize an idea, grasp it, and understand it." Is all of that **comprehensible** to you?

Scrupulously: What is a **scruple**? First of all it is a very nice word to know. A **scruple** is a tiny, but maybe sharp, bit of stone. Have you ever had a **scruple** in your shoe? Of course, and therefore you know perfectly well that for all its small size a scruple in your shoe can be very irritating, and might even prevent you from walking. Perhaps the most famous **scruple**, at least in fairy tales, was the pea that kept that princess awake despite all those mattresses placed between herself and that pea. In other words, a **scruple**, for all its tiny size, can have a powerful effect. When you use the term **scrupulous**, as for example when you tell your teacher that you most **scrupulously** did your homework the night before, you mean that you concentrated on every tiny detail of what you did, leaving no **scruple** of error that might cause you to get less than an A.

Greenwich Village: A part of New York City, around Washington Square, which has always been a favorite address for artists and writers. In spite of its being in the heart of such a big city, the area preserves the atmosphere of a village, and one with marvelous little cafes, bookshops, boutiques, and artist's studios. It is a fun place to visit, and one might one day live there, and write some great poetry like e e cummings.

FROST

Wrested: Now here is a word that is not from Latin, but from the Middle or Old English word *wresten*, which meant "to wrestle, or struggle." Now you know what a "wrestler" really is. Does it not make sense that the verb **to wrest**, as we use it, means to grab or struggle with a certain force to get something? In my use of the word, New England being famous for its hard and rocky soil, you had to really struggle **to wrest** a living from the land.

Questing: You all know this word because knights in shining armor always went **questing**. Name three famous **quests**, please. On the other hand, never mind. As for myself I think immediately of the "**Quest** for the Holy Grail" by Sir Galahad, "The **Quest** for the Golden Fleece" by the Argonauts, and . . . well, you name the third and write it here:

_____.

In any case **a quest** is more than just a search, although if you want to be rather poetic about it you could, after all, go **questing** for your lost pencil. Generally, however, the implication is usually of a long, adventurous and heroic search for some noble great cause, maybe to win the hand of a fair lady, or to gain riches and honor. And don't forget: School is a **quest** for knowledge which you wrest from your books with the help of your teachers.

STEVENS

Tapestry: A heavy cloth, like a rug, woven with decorative designs. The most famous so-called **tapestry** of the western world is the **Bayeux Tapestry**, which is only 20 inches high, but 230 feet long. It was woven to depict the Battle of Hastings, fought Oct. 14th, 1066, when William "the Conqueror," who had crossed the English Channel from Normandy, defeated the Saxon King Harold. This particular **tapestry** is more like an embroidered cloth less thick than we generally think a **tapestry** is, but it has survived for almost 1000 years. It shows King Harold being shot by an arrow in the eye, but probably he died of innumerable spear wounds. The fact that the designer chose to emphasize the arrow in the eye demonstrates that even then "the media," in this case the medium not of television but of woven cloth, emphasized the most dramatic element of a news item.

Juxtapositions: The plural, obviously, of **juxtaposition**. _Juxta_, or _iuxta_ (because Latin does not have a J in its alphabet, and uses an I instead) means "near" or "beside." Therefore what, pray tell, does "juxtaposition" mean?

Pooh-bah: To "pooh" is to make that nonverbal gesture of blowing or puffing or maybe even tut-tutting something away. The action dismisses whatever is being pooh-poohed as being not even worth real words. The term Pooh-bah comes from a character in Gilbert and Sullivan's famous comic opera, _The Mikado_ (1885), a ruler who was all puffed up with his self-importance. Another famous Pooh-bah was Mr. Toad in _The Wind and the Willows_.

Inchlings: An invented word for a tiny person. The Lilliputians, I think, must have been **inchlings**. Didn't they tie someone up? Who? Please put his name in this space:

_____

Caftan: Here is a word we get from Arabia, their _qaftan_, one of a few that have entered the English language. A caftan is a long robe with wide sleeves, fastened at the waist by a belt. **Caftans** were popular in the 1970s, but I looked ridiculous in a "flowing robe" when I tried one, hoping to look "cool," and I gave it up immediately when my wife burst out laughing. Perhaps if I had had a camel...?

Henna: A shrub cultivated in Egypt, from which is extracted a reddish-orangey-tangerineish-vermiliony-crimsonish-brownie-umberish dye.

Hackles: in Middle English a _hatchel_ was a special comb with iron teeth for picking out the finer fibers of flax to make linen threads and clothing. Linen, a cool, durable, and comfortable cloth, remains popular today. In the Metropolitan Museum in New York you can see a linen shirt that was made over three thousand years ago. A **hackle**, therefore, is something that resembles a *hatchel,* that is, anything that stands forth or sticks out, like the teeth of a comb. The long feathers at the neck of a peacock or rooster are called **hackles**. When a dog growls in fear and anger, it "gets its **hackles** up," the hair on the back of its neck standing on end. A fisherman who ties a fly with little tufts of feathers that stick out like an insect's wings is making a **hackle fly**. Have you ever had the hair on the back of your neck tingle and stand up a little bit? Have your **hackles** ever got up when you have been suddenly frightened?

Suffice: To be enough, to satisfy a need. **To suffice** is, of course, the verb, **sufficient** the adjective, **sufficiently** the adverb. A **sufficient** amount of homework, **sufficiently** well done, will **suffice** to get you a passing grade. Stevens is saying something very interesting here, namely that it is through our own highly individual ways of thinking and seeing the world, through what he calls "the poetry of the mind," that we create for ourselves ways of dealing with our surroundings that will **suffice**.

AIKEN

Mellifluous (muh-LIFF-loo-us): Whenever you see a word beginning with "mel" or "mellis," you can pretty much count on something sweet happening next. This is because *mel, mellis* means "honey" in Latin. *Fluere* means to flow, like a fluid. Therefore, if in English you say something that flows from the tongue sweetly and smoothly, like honey, and sounds equally so to the listener's ear, you are speaking **mellifluously**. On Mother's Day you might say something **mellifluous** to your Mom, and then ask her if she can spell it.

Debussy: Claude Debussy (1862-1918) was a famous French composer, renowned for making music that combined brilliant juxtapositions of notes and chords into pieces that are wonderfully fluid, indeed mellifluous, like honey to the ear.

Lyrical: Think of a lyre, that little harp-like instrument that was popular in ancient Greece, and which was called a *Lyra.* Harps of any sort, of course, are famous for making mellifluous sounds. The sound of each string flows so beautifully into the sound of the next that it is said you cannot make an "ugly" sound on a harp. When anything, whether it be music, a poem, or a passage of literature, is described as **lyrical**, it means that it has a beautiful, light, and free-flowing quality. A **lyric**, by the way, has a more specific meaning, and generally means the words written to accompany a song. While we are at it, a "libretto" is the name for the words that accompany some great, long musical composition, such as an opera.

NASH

Panache (puh-NOSH): The "ache" in this word is not pronounced like the "ache" in "ear Ache." The "che" should sound like the "sh" in "hush," and **panache** rhymes with bosh. It comes from an old French word, *pennache*, which itself came from the Latin *penna*, meaning a feather. I think it interesting that a *penni* is, or was, also a Finnish (Quick, where is Finland on the map?) coin of tiny value. Therefore have it whichever way you want it: when you are "penniless" you have neither a penny nor a feather to your name. As for **panache**, that word implies that whoever has it possesses a dashing style and elegance of manner, as when you stick a feather in your cap. Who tried to assume this manner, as he rode to town, by doing just that and calling it "macaroni"?

Unique: *Uniqus* in Latin means "single." In fact, it truly means " the one and only." When something is **unique** there is NO OTHER like it. Therefore, and please mind this now, for you are really about to learn something, you must never say that something is "very **unique**," because it will demonstrate that you do not really know the meaning of **unique**. Unique does not mean rare. It goes beyond even very rare. It is the ONLY. Putting the word "very" in front of it is altogether unnecessary.

Prolific: Fruitful, producing many offspring. When something is **proliferating** it is reproducing rapidly, making lots of new buds, blooms, rabbits, words, etc. A **prolific** author writes a lot of books. Nash's **prolific** pen produced many poems.

Panjandrum: This is the same as a Pooh-bah, but dates well before *The Mikado*. **Panjandrum** comes from a nonsense story written in 1755 by one Samuel Foote. I have no idea how he came up with the name. If you would research the topic, and write a thesis of at least 150 closely written pages, with footnotes, you might get a Ph.D. even before you reached the eighth grade. As for Archibald MacLeish, he was neither a Pooh-bah nor a **Panjandrum**, that is to say he was not puffed up, or in any way a blow-hard like Mr. Toad. He was a highly respected gentleman of letters, and a poet of great distinction, who won the Pulitzer Prize for Poetry in 1932. In his case, I call him a **panjandrum** out of respect, if rather playfully. One can, after all, "play" with words. On the other hand, there are many actors and actresses, and other types of "talking heads" on television who are, indeed **panjandrums** in the less generous sense of the word.

SPENDER

Totalitarian (toe-tal-ih-TAIR-ee-un): Note the "total" in this word, which hints at its meaning. **Totalitarian** is generally applied to those forms of government that have total control over their citizens. In the twentieth century the famous, or rather infamous, governments led by Mussolini in Italy, Hitler in Germany, Stalin in Russia, and Mao Tse-tung in China were archetypal **totalitarian** governments. Unlike democracies, which believe in the worth and power of each individual, **totalitarian** governments regarded individual worth as having value only in the service of the greater needs of the state or country.

"Up to": It seems to me, but I may be wrong, that once upon a time English students went **up to** Oxford, but "down to Cambridge." Or was it the other way around? In any case, and rather strangely it seems to me, I do not think that going "up" or "down" had any relationship to traveling north or south, any more that it does when we speak of going "down south" or "up north."

THOMAS

Magnitude: *Magna* means "greatness," coming to us (yet again!) from Latin, and **magnitude** means size or extent, but often referring to "bigness." What, just to test you, was the Magna Carta? Why is it such an honor to graduate *Magna cum Laude*? Astronomers describe the brightness of stars as being of this or that **magnitude**. Sirius, in the constellation of Orion, is the brightest star in the sky, and is described as being of the First **Magnitude**. Everything has a certain **magnitude**, from great to small. If you get As all the time, you will graduate *Magna cum Laude*, which in Latin means "greatly with praise."

Celtic: This word is generally pronounced like "Keltic," but some people say it should be

"Seltic." You will have to take your pick. In any case, the Celts (how DID you pronounce it, by the way?) were an early pre-historic people who first lived on the western shores of Europe and then in large numbers emigrated to the British Islands. They were themselves pushed farther and farther back, into the highlands of Scotland and Wales, and across the Irish Sea to Ireland, by the Angles and Saxons, other invaders from what is now Germany. In these remote places, the Celts continued to live according to their ancient cultural beliefs. They were brilliant artisans, creating elaborate and very beautiful designs with which they embellished their utensils, shields, swords, and helmets. They possessed a gift for music, poetry, and speaking. Still today, people of Celtic origin, the Irish, the highland Scots, and the Welsh, possess and practice these gifts. You have but to listen to a Welshman's voice, or hear an Irish lass sing, or be stirred by the sound of the Scottish bagpipes to realize how wonderfully the talents of the **Celts** have been preserved. Thomas not only was famous for his poetry, but for the rich sound of his voice when he read his poems.

Incandescent: *Candela* in Latin means a candle. Anything that is **incandescent** glows with a bright, white-hot light. A burning candle, of course, is not really white-hot, but one must remember that once upon a time, before the **incandescent** light bulb came along, it was the nearest thing people had to that pure, white light we enjoy now. In terms of magnitude, for certain, the sun is the most **incandescent** giver of light and heat. When someone is really "hot," be they a poet or a baseball player, you can think of them, as I have here, as **incandescent**.

Flamboyant: A *flambeau* in French is a torch. The flame of a torch flares up and down, moving intricately in the breeze, the flames flickering around and about each other. Is your eye not caught up by seeing a fire burn? Anything that is **flamboyant** catches one's eye and attention. A **flamboyant** person is showy, or flashy, in dress or manner. On the "Magnitude Scale of **Flamboyance**" the shy Mr. Peepers would be a one, and Dylan Thomas a ten, particularly when he was in a bar drinking.

Resonant: This word comes from the Latin word meaning "echo." When you shout at the mountains, and hear returned the deep, rich, resounding echo of your words reverberating among the hills, making your voice seem so much bigger than it is, your voice has been made **resonant**. Sound studios have devices that make a singer's voice more **resonant** than it might naturally be. But some people are born with deep **resonant** voices all of their own, and Thomas was one of these.

Luxurious: *Luxus* in Latin means soft-living, and quite more soft than is actually necessary for simple survival in a hard world. It is, for example, a bit of a luxury to have a soft pillow for your head at night rather than a stone. It is more of a luxury to drive around in a Lexus (even the name of that car sounds like what?) than an ox cart, with the ox angry at having to do all the pulling. And what about, for crossing oceans, a great, magnificently appointed yacht as opposed to a leaking rowboat? Anything that is **luxurious** is usually rich in quality, but it does not necessarily mean it has to be flamboyant either. Words, too, can be used either sparingly or luxuriously, or even flamboyantly, as Thomas was also very capable of doing in his poetry.

Luxuriant: Having to do with vegetation and its profuse growth. You might say, as you regarded a particularly productive field of broccoli, "What a **luxuriant** crop of broccoli. I can't wait to eat it for dinner tonight!" On the other hand, you would never call broccoli "luxurious," would you? Beyond broccoli, cabbage, ferns, grass and other plants that might grow luxu-

riantly, the word can also be applied to speech of a rich and florid sort. Some writers incline toward a spare use of words. Others, like Thomas, revel in the opportunity to use all manner of them in bright new combinations, each word in its abundance tumbling upon the next, the reader himself being caught up, magically in the poetry of Dylan Thomas, in their **luxuriant, fruitful profusion.**

Poignant (POIN-yant): Anything that is **poignant** is sharp to the taste or smell, but beyond that it is also keen and sharply painful to the feelings: it strikes to the heart, like a dagger. Aha! The French word for a dagger is a *poignard*, pronounced poin-yard, as **poignant** is pronounced poin-yant. If you take the test at the end of this course and do terribly, missing every single question, I, your teacher, will be **poignantly** stricken, as though by a dagger.

SEUSS

High-fallutin': I remember reading in *Time* magazine years ago about some flamboyant person who was described as being 'rootin', tootin', rip-snortin', quick- shootin', and **high-fallutin'**. Strung together, they describe a very flamboyant person. They are all colloquialisms, words that we commonly and informally use, but which may not even be found in a dictionary. Our speech is full of colloquialisms, which add fun and flavor to our ability to communicate. As for **high-fallutin'**, it implies to me anyone who tends to put on fancy airs, manners, or clothing, and then goes "astruttin'."

MOORE

Anthologist: The Greek word *anthos* means flower. *Logos* means "word" in Latin. Aha! An **anthology** is therefore a collection of "flower-words," or more accurately a selection of poems and stories, not necessarily all written by the same author, but picked (like flowers) by some **anthologist** and brought together not in a vase but a book. When choosing these "flowers of literature," the **anthologist** gets to pick what he or she likes best.

Dauntlessly: To **daunt** is to make afraid. To be dauntless is to not be made afraid. To do something **dauntlessly** is to do it fearlessly. One of my favorite airplanes when I was a boy during World War Two was the Douglas **"Dauntless,"** a dive bomber. A few **Dauntless** bombers most dramatically, even flamboyantly, sank Japan's aircraft carriers at the Battle of Midway in the Pacific Ocean in May, 1942.

Sensual: Having to do with the body or senses as opposed to the mind or intellect. **Sensual** pleasures may, in fact, be even voluptuous, which is a word you either know or may look up in the dictionary under V.

EPILOGUE

Q.E.D.: An abbreviation that stands for *Quod erat demonstrandum,* meaning "which has been demonstrated," and by which letters Roman authors and geometers would conclude their written presentations, having brought their argument to its final dignified, as opposed to high-fallutin', conclusion. And by that I conclude this Glossary: Q.E.D..

ARTISTS

- 4   AL, Ali Lewis, 7th Grade
- 3   AM, Alex Mixon, 8th
- 4   AP, Adriana Piekarewicz, 8th
- 2   AR, Austin Russell, 8th
- 4   AS (Poe), Adam Shepherd, 8th
- 3   AS (Whitman), Ashton Shippy, 7th
- 4   AW, Andre Weeks, 7th
- 4   BB, Ben Butler, 7th
- 4   CE, Caroline Eubanks, 6th
- 4   CS, Conor Sweeney, 6th
- 4   HD, Holden Dickson, 8th
- 4   JA, Jordan Anderson, 8th
- 4   JH, Jordan Hoffman, 7th
- 4   JM, Jenny Moore, 8th
- 4   JP, Jordan Palmer, 7th
- 3   KB, Kathleen Bennett, 8th
- 4   LD, LIndsey Dee, 7th
- 4   LL, Liz Landers, 6th
- 4   MB, Madison Bateman, 6th
- 4   MCS, Mary Crit Smith, 6th
- 4   MG, Meghan Gould, 6th
- 3   MW, Mary Watkins, 7th
- 2   PC, Pierce Cassedy, 7th
- 3   RM, Reed McCord, 7th
- 4   SLB, Sarah Logan Beasley, 6th
- 4   SN, Susumu Noda, 8th
- 4   SP, Stephanie Post, 6th
- 4   SW, Spencer Walker, 6th
- 4   WL, Will Liner, 6th